Raising a *Lady* IN *Waiting*

Mother's Workbook

RAISING A *Lady* IN *Waiting*

MOTHER'S WORKBOOK

JACKIE KENDALL

DESTINY IMAGE® PUBLISHERS, INC.

P.O. Box 310, Shippensburg, PA 17257-0310

"Promoting Inspired Lives."

This book and all other Destiny Image, Revival Press, MercyPlace, Fresh Bread, Destiny Image Fiction, and Treasure House books are available at Christian bookstores and distributors worldwide.

For a U.S. bookstore nearest you, call 1-800-722-6774.

For more information on foreign distributors, call 717-532-3040.

Reach us on the Internet: www.destinyimage.com.

ISBN 13 TP: 978-0-7684-0366-4

For Worldwide Distribution, Printed in the U.S.A.

1 2 3 4 5 6 7 8 / 17 16 15 14 13

CONTENTS

A MESSAGE TO THE MOMS

*M*om, you're up!

While I want to encourage you to re-read the preface to the book (or read it for the first time, if you have not opened your book yet), a reminder never hurts!

The wonderful thing about going through *Raising a Lady in Waiting* in this format, and what you can expect from me along the journey ahead, is this: authenticity and experience. I know where you've been and I want to coach you, drawing from my personal history, on how to raise a lady in waiting. To raise up young women who wait for God's Boaz and avoid Bozos like the plague, it is so important, Mom, that you understand your role as your daughter's greatest coach and number one cheerleader. Get out the pom poms!

I'm amazed at the skewed perspective so many parents have adopted when it comes to schools. Even church and Sunday school! Seriously, it makes me want to scream: *You are the person God has chosen to raise your daughter! It is no one else's responsibility!* This perspective is motivated by downright laziness. Now with school and church, there are positives to the investment they make in our kids, but it gets ugly when we incorporate media and television into the mix. Basically, we want to give our children to other people and places so that they will "raise" them for us. Then we wonder why our kids end up making some of the decisions they do—namely, our daughters dating Bozo guys instead of waiting for God's Boaz.

9

This *study* is designed to help you connect with your daughter in a way that few mothers do, and, I pray, be a stepping-stone toward a much more honest, open, and authentic relationship between the two of you. Believe me, you are going to need it when Bozo comes a-knocking. Whether you have a great relationship already with no secrets or you feel closed off from one another, like you two are living on different planets—my prayer is that by going through this book and workbook together, something special takes place in your relationship.

Okay, so I am not one to be vague. The "something special" I want to see happen is *you* become your daughter's teacher, cheerleader, coach, and spiritual monitor (I'll explain this later on in the book!). Your kids might not come out and say it, but according to an extensive study conducted by *USA Today Weekend Magazine*, 70 percent of 272,400 polled teenagers identified their parents as the most important influence in your lives. Wow! Not media. Not peers. Not school. Not church. Yeah, *you* Mom!

Like I said at the beginning, *Mom, you're up*. If these statistics are true, you have an awesome and exciting opportunity standing before you.

Here is what I would like you to do next: *Read the preface to Raising a Lady in Waiting*. It gives you a glimpse of my personal story, and also shares the reason why I believe this message is so important for moms to share with their daughters. Then you will begin your interactive journey alongside your daughter. You will read the book, and she will read the book. You will fill out your workbook, and then she will fill out her workbook. You will do the readings and exercises separately, only because I expect both of you are tremendously busy.

That said, we cannot bow down at the altar of busyness. It can become a god if we are not careful. At the end of each week, you and your daughter will come together for a time of sharing, mentorship, and authentic relationship building. You will have the opportunity to talk, openly and honestly, about the topic you both studied that week and share anything from your workbook experience that might help your daughter along the journey to becoming a *lady in waiting*.

Above all, Mom, my prayer is that your young lady in waiting would be a pursuer of the Lord Jesus Christ *above all else*. As He is the most important relationship in her life, I can assure you, everything else will come into its place. She will need coaching along the way, absolutely. We all do through this journey. That said, when your young lady is first and foremost one sold out to King Jesus, it will become *very difficult* for her to give her heart away to *anyone* who treats her in a way that her King would disapprove of.

Here's to the journey ahead. I'm so thrilled. So excited. So expectant that a great God is going to do great things in both of your lives!

Much love,

Jackie

HOW TO USE THIS WORKBOOK

Here are some tips on how to use this workbook for yourself, work with your daughter through the chapters of the book/workbook sessions, and get the most out of this experience that you possibly can.

A NOTE ON THE TIME COMMITMENT...

When it comes to the time commitment required, I stress *quality over quantity*. I know you are both busy people. *You* are busy taking care of a family, raising children, having a career, going to school—all of those things that you as a mom and a woman need to be doing.

I'm also confident that your daughter has a rather healthy social calendar, where friends, school, sports, shopping, and all of those other things may be taking up a good portion of her time.

The exercises in this workbook should not take you more than 15-20 minutes per day. Again, it is so important that in spite of our busyness, we do not sacrifice the most important things at the altar of the myriad of little things demanding our time. The investment in your child is one of the most precious and important things you can devote your time to. Consider that when it comes to doing this study.

BREAKDOWN

Weekly Video Coaching Tip from Jackie

If possible, watch this together—mom and daughter. If not, both of you can watch it separately, but it would be best for you to watch the clip together. For about five minutes, I am going to *coach* you on what to expect in that week's session, and what you should expect to get out of it—mom *and* daughter. I will leave you with an *encouragement*. It might be in the form of a testimony. Maybe it will be a life lesson I have learned along the journey, or a testimony someone shared with me. After watching this, you will be ready to take on the week!

Daily Readings from Raising a Lady in Waiting

Read your daily segment(s) from *Raising a Lady in Waiting* as provided in each session. This will help you go through the book at a comfortable pace and digest all the major concepts and principles that are presented. Every day, you will be assigned to read a certain section of the chapter and answer daily reflection questions.

Each chapter will be broken into five daily sections. It is recommended that you do the readings/daily discussion questions on Monday through Friday, so that you can devote one of the weekend days to spend time with your daughter and review the material you covered. While this specific schedule is not essential, we find that this particular method tends to work best to promote the overall goal of the exercises.

Daily Reflection Questions

Each section will have corresponding Daily Reflection Questions designed to get you interacting with the material. These questions will actually coincide with what your daughter is reading and responding to in her workbook.

The goal is that you will: 1) read the book, 2) go through the workbook activities, and 3) at the end of the week, be able to have an honest, open, real discussion about what you have been going through in the workbook.

Daily Prayer for Mother and Daughter

Principles without prayer are just informational tidbits. Prayer adds substance and power to what we are doing here. I want you, Mom, to be praying for God's wisdom to shape you as your daughter's mentor, and also to shape your daughter in the process.

Also, keep in mind these prayers are designed to help, not hinder, your personal prayer life. In other words, we want to give you some type of template to pray, not to be the be-all and end-all of your prayer life, but as something to jump-start your prayer focus for the day, specifically relating to your daughter. We must be focused in our prayers, especially when it comes to our children.

Mother-Daughter time

At the end of the week, preferably on Saturday or Sunday, Mom, you need to get with your daughter and spend some time together. Maybe grab lunch somewhere or coffee. This exercise is not designed to be some cold, distant, "What do *you* learn about?" Okay. Got it. Now, "What did *you* learn about going through this book?" Okay. Cool. Are we done now? Time to go off to separate ends of life again.

Perhaps other devotionals and books have created such a stagnant climate in the past, but quite honestly, I didn't have the time to present this material so that moms and daughters just made it another "must do" on the list. You are going through this material because you recognize the *value* and the *investment*.

I am going to present this material in a very simple way for you to use it however you feel comfortable. Basically, I am giving you a set of questions for both you and your daughter to answer. If either of you don't feel like you can answer a certain question, fear not! Answer it based on what you *think* would be the right answer after going through that section in *Raising a Lady in Waiting*. Mom, you may not have all of the answers and that is totally cool. None of us do! Use this time to talk. Talk about what you read. Talk about some of the exercises you went through. Were they a struggle? Where there certain questions that you could not answer? Were there questions that you could answer and *were excited* about the answer? I am leery of giving *too much* structure here, as this needs to be organic and real. Again, I'll simply provide you a list of questions to help guide your discussion. The rest is up to you!

INTRODUCTION SESSION

Lady in Waiting is not about finding the right man,
but becoming the right woman.

The *Lady in Waiting*
recklessly abandons herself to the
Lordship of Christ,
diligently uses her single days,
trusts God with unwavering faith,
demonstrates virtue in daily life,
loves God with undistracted devotion,
stands for physical and emotional purity,
lives in security,
responds to life in contentment,
makes choices based on her convictions,
and waits patiently for
God to meet her needs.

INTRODUCTION

Read: *RALIW* Introduction, pages 21-23 (Read up
until the *Ideal Mom, Former Prostitute* heading.)

---

*T*he principles in this book are intended to
guard and to guide: To guard your daughter
from a Bozo guy and to guide her toward a
man worth waiting for—a modern Boaz.

DAILY REFLECTION QUESTIONS

1. In general, why do you believe it is so important to guard your
    daughter from a "Bozo" guy?

He is going to be a guy with poor character,
selfish, self absorbed. The kind of guy who
is looking for a good time not a long time.
Who ever you marry impacts your life in every
way until death do you part.

2. When you read the phrase, "Bozo" guy, what does that mean to you?

• a guy who shows up with his pants hanging down
with his boxers hanging out, hat on side ways
saying whatz up! no seriously someone who
is imature, very shallow, selfish, no direction
or purpose in life.

3. How does the man whom your daughter ends up with—either a Bozo or a Boaz—actually determine the course of your daughter's future?

The two become one. Bozo is not going to love, encourage, cherrish his wife. Boaz is going to respect my daughter, honor her, want the best for her, take care of her needs, lead her, love her.

DAILY PRAYER

Father, help me to guard my daughter from second-bests and guide her toward embracing Your good and perfect plan for her life. Give me wisdom on how to mentor her using these principles in the days and weeks ahead.

And Holy Spirit, as (Daughter's Name) is reading through this book too, open her heart to hear Your voice and stir her to also pursue Your perfect plan for her life.

In Jesus' Name, Amen.

IDEAL MOM—FORMER PROSTITUTE

Read: *RALIW* Introduction, page 23 (Read the
Ideal Mom—Former Prostitute section.)

If by any chance you are a mom who thinks it
is too late—be encouraged. The breath in your
nostrils is proof of the hope that God is not
finished with you or your daughter yet.

DAILY REFLECTION QUESTIONS

1. Go on to read about Rahab in Joshua 2. This former prostitute
would become the mother of Boaz, the leading man in the love story of Ruth. What messages does Rahab's story speak to a mom who
believes she has messed up beyond fixing or has made one too many
poor choices in her life?

There is always hope. God doesn't
forsake even those who make a
mess of their lives

2. How does this specifically speak to you as a mom?

There is always hope even when
things feel hopeless.

_____

_____

_____

DAILY PRAYER

Lord, thank You for Your grace. You are the God of second chances, and third chances...and one-thousandth chances. Nothing exhausts Your grace, Your mercy, and Your kindness. I confess, I have made mistakes in the past. I may be making them right now. Instead of giving up, I push forward. I reject the enemy's lie that it is "too late." The fact that I am alive and breathing means there is hope that You are not finished with me or my daughter.

Fill (Daughter's Name) with hope that You have amazing plans for her, even if she feels like she has messed up beyond forgiveness. Expose that lie to her and enable her to break free from condemnation. And Lord, empower me to reveal Your overwhelming grace and kindness to her as we move forward in this journey together.

In Jesus' Name, Amen.

VITAL COLLEGE PREP COURSE

Read: *RALIW* Introduction, pages 23-24 (Read
the *Vital College Prep Course* section.)

I know too many kids who are passing school
and flunking life in their relationships.

DAILY REFLECTION QUESTIONS

1. Why do you think so many of our daughters (yes, even those who go
    to Christian schools and are attending church) are making such un-
    wise and horrible choices in their everyday lives?

    They are being influenced by their peers,
    tv, society. Parents have checked out.
    They are not doing the job of training
    up their child. Proverbs 22:6

2. What does this statement mean to you: "Too many kids are passing
    school and flunking life in their relationships"?

    We are becoming a disconnected,
    isolated society through technology.
    families are divorced, relationships
    are not being mentored + developed.

3. Why it is important that you, as a mom, do more than just buy your daughter this book, but actually model the principles on a daily basis?

Words and actions go together.
I have to be actively involved
in my girls lives, their interests,
and friendships.

DAILY PRAYER

Lord, help me not to be ignorant to what is going on in the next generation—especially in my daughter.

I pray for (Daughter's Name), that You would protect her from the poor choices available to her daily, and that You would enable me to model these heart-preserving principles to her. I don't want to just get her a book. I don't want to just tell her to "do this" or "don't do this." Father, help me to live this out before her eyes. Above all, may my growing love and passion for You make (Daughter's Name) hungry for what I have.

In Jesus' Name, Amen.

"CLIFF NOTES" FOR MOM

Read: *RALIW* Introduction, pages 24-25
(Read the *Cliff Notes for Mom* section.)

You can consider this the "Cliff Notes" from my
decades of searching for transferrable concepts to help
mothers raise girls who will not become Bozo magnets.

DAILY REFLECTION QUESTIONS

1. Just as I have written this book out of my past experience, learning a thing or two about judging the difference between a Boaz and a Bozo, I think it is very important for you to stop and consider your personal "cliff notes." Think of past situations in your life where you were pursued by a Bozo. Did you end up giving in to the pursuit? Why or why not?

   Sometimes I did. At 15 I made a vow to not pursue pointless boys. I wanted to wait for my future husband. Interestingly, I met my hubby shortly after this vow!

   Note: Should you feel directed by the Holy Spirit to share this with your daughter, your personal history of experience is very important in helping her navigate the relationship decisions she is making today.

2. Where is your daughter right now, in terms of being attracted to the opposite sex? Is she not interested yet and boys are still *gross*? Is she "crushing" on a boy at school? Is she currently in a relationship? Has her heart already been broken by a Bozo? It is essential that you are able to accurately identify where she is so you can most effectively communicate these principles with her.

DAILY PRAYER

Lord, help me to discern where my daughter is on her journey and begin to use Your wisdom to share with her principles that will help her to make godly decisions in the years to come.

In Jesus' Name, Amen.

GUIDEBOOK FOR PARIS...
AND PARENTING

Read: *RALIW* Introduction, pages 25-29 (Read the
Guidebook for Paris and Parenting section, take your *Prep
Quiz for Moms*, and read the information that follows.)

I feel like this book will be a helpful tour guidebook

as you maneuver through the challenges of raising

a Young Lady in Waiting and avoiding the tyranny

of a precious child becoming a Bozo magnet.

DAILY REFLECTION QUESTIONS

1. Why is it important to keep your daughter's standards high, even if
    you believe you are raising a "good girl"?

    temptation will come at some point.
    Even when "Mr. right" comes into
    the picture it is important to be
    strong

    Before moving on, I recommend doing the *Daily Prayer* and then
    turning over to the *Prep Quiz for Moms*.

DAILY PRAYER

Lord, prepare my heart to answer the following questions transparently and honestly. Whether I score well or poorly, I refuse to get disheartened and feel like a failure. May encouragement or discouragement help me to have a teachable heart so that in the weeks to come, I can receive Your wisdom through the principles I will be learning.

Thank You, Father, that I am learning how to invest in my daughter and strengthen her standards.

And above all, help me to keep my eyes fixed on Jesus, the Unchanging One. I cannot be attached to the outcome of my child's/children's lives, but I am attached to Jesus and I am so thankful He remains the Rock of security no matter what life brings.

In the weeks to come, help my daughter to increase her trust and confidence in Jesus, that He would be her Rock and unchanging source of strength.

In Jesus' Name, Amen.

PREP QUIZ
FOR MOMS

Key Question: *Am I prepared to raise a Young Lady in Waiting?* (Can I help prevent my daughter from marrying a Bozo?)

1.   Do you know why older guys date younger girls?

2.   Is your daughter growing in her love for Jesus, and does she see such growth in you?

3.   Is your daughter experienced in doing for others? Does she help out at home and at church? Does she see this type of diligence in her mom, who is her first role model?

4.   What is keeping your teen from doing for others? Is your teen too self-focused? Does she only do for others when it benefits her in the long run?

5.   Does your teen have a No-Bozo Heart Guard? Does she understand the significance of getting her "seven" daily? (See Romans 10:17.)

6.   Mom, did you know that sex ruins a good relationship or sustains a bad one?

7.   Mom, did you know that that girls play at sex to get love and boys play at love to get sex?

8.   Does your daughter grasp that if she will continue to pursue God's heart, she will attract someone who will encourage her to continue

to grow—and they will be each other's spiritual cheerleaders? (See Hebrews 10:24.)

9. Mom, do you know what the "No Zone" is? Does your teen know about the "No Zone" and about staying out of it?

10. Mom, do you know why teen girls go too far? Would you know how to explain the law of diminishing returns to your daughter and her friends?

11. Do you know why so many precious girls marry Bozo guys? Did you know that sex blinds a girl to the Bozo she is dating or attracted to?

12. Do you know your daughter's "love tank" level? If her earthly father is absent, that love tank needs supernatural filling by her heavenly Father. Secure in Jesus, He must fill her heart deficit.

13. Is your teenager mildly content or an incessant whiner? Me-centric girls are "Bozo bait"—one selfish teen attracting another and wanting instant gratification.

14. Do you know how to be a "spiritual monitor" of your daughter's "crushing" on guys?

15. Does your teen carry (in her wallet or on her cell phone) a list of the qualities that describe Mr. Right?

16. Does your teen know how to avoid wearing chains on her wedding day? (See Second Corinthians 6:14.)

17. How patient is your teen? Waiting is a prerequisite for a "man worth waiting for"; impatience is the easiest way to be Bozo bait. (Worse than waiting is wishing you had!)

MOTHER/DAUGHTER SESSION

INSTRUCTIONS

You have both gone through the introduction in both the book and workbook. Here are some of the questions you can discuss during your first mother-daughter session:

- What does Jackie mean when she talks about a "Bozo" guy versus a Boaz?

- What does the story of Rahab the prostitute say to you about the people God uses to do great things?

- Why is it so important to keep high standards?

- What are some of the things that culture, society, and other people say about women who have high standards?

- Deep down, do you think that women with high standards are ultimately looked down on or admired (even if they are secretly admired)?

- What are some of the benefits of keeping your standards high and not giving in to compromise?

- What did you think of the prep quiz?

- Were there certain questions that didn't make sense? If so, which ones? (Most likely, these are the questions that used phrases we will be talking about in the weeks ahead.)

RAISING A YOUNG LADY OF RECKLESS ABANDON

As daughters of the King who gave Himself for us, we are to give ourselves to Him, leaving the world, giving up our strategies, and withdrawing support from the wiles of the devil and the ways of the flesh. Reckless abandon is how we fling ourselves toward God and utterly forsake our sinful nature.

THE "SHOUT YES" MOM

Read: *RALIW* Chapter 1, pages 31-33 (Read *Ruth's
Reckless Abandon* and *The Shout Yes Mom* sections.)

*S*aying "Yes" to God is an act of daily surrender
and a display of one's own reckless abandon.

DAILY REFLECTION QUESTIONS

1. What does reckless abandon look like to God? Consider the example
   of Ruth and Naomi. How did Ruth demonstrate reckless abandon to
   God, and how can you follow her example in your life?

   Surrendering of self, pride, agenda, purpose,
   plans, dreams, goals. and saying yes
   to God's purpose, plans goals.

2. How do you model a "Shout Yes" lifestyle to God—before
   your daughter?

   - being obedient to God's calling.
   - being in the word regularly.
   - living by faith not by sight.
   - living counter cultural

3. How do you envision your daughter being one who says "Yes" to God?

only God can transform each of us. I can teach, model, and pray for my daughter. She has to desire to say "yes" to God, and then put her words into action by doing.

DAILY PRAYER

May my life shout yes to You, Jesus. Every decision, every thought, every attitude and action—I pray that they would say "Yes" to Your will, Your plan, and Your purpose.

Lord, may my reckless abandon to You speak to my daughter. May it model a lifestyle that she is hungry to walk in and experience as her own. I pray she would see that the obedience of a "Shout Yes" lifestyle releases Your blessing and Your purpose in way that satisfies beyond anything else.

In Jesus' Name, Amen.

OUR DAUGHTERS—GOD'S VESSELS

Read: *RALIW* Chapter 1, pages 34-37 (Read *Dateless Friday Night Miracles* and *Maddie and Libby's Story* sections.)

---

*R*eckless abandon is a level of surrender that unlocks the greatest treasures God has in store for His kids.

DAILY REFLECTION QUESTIONS

1. Based on what Jackie experienced during her *Dateless Friday Night Miracle*, what are some benefits to saying "No" to certain things and "Yes" to God?

   You are in the will of God for your life. God becomes the center of everything you do. You save yourself from needless pain / heartache.

2. Can you tell if your daughter is growing spiritually? What are some noticeable signs of her spiritual growth? Are there signs that reflect the opposite—that she is not growing spiritually?

   Slow and steady growth. Alyssa right now could use some more spiritual growth. God has not grabbed her whole heart. I believe He will though.

EKRaising a *Lady* in *Waiting* Daughter's Workbook

3. What are you personally doing to *passionately* encourage your daughter's relationship with the Lord? If you aren't doing anything or seem to be doing the wrong things—start with prayer!

praying, encouraging, discipling, mentoring, allowing her to be a part of christian activities, environment Proverbs 22:6 train up your child in the way they should go, when they are old they will not depart from it.

DAILY PRAYER

Lord, help me to keep the first things first in prayer. When it comes to praying for (Daughter's Name), may my most important focus be her passionate relationship with You. Show me how I can encourage her in pursuing You above everything else—not religiously, not using a bunch of rules, regulations, and laws. Show me how to help stir her hunger for You, King Jesus. I know this is the job of the Holy Spirit. But I also know that You use normal people like me to work with You to accomplish great things.

In His Name, Amen.

YOUR DAUGHTER: PREGNANT WITH MESSIAH

Read: *RALIW* Chapter 1, page 38 (Read *Your Daughter Pregnant with Messiah!* section.)

The safest place for your girl to be is the place where she is more concerned about what God thinks than what anybody else thinks.

DAILY REFLECTION QUESTIONS

1. How have you observed your daughter saying "Yes" to God with reckless abandon? List examples of times when your daughter has obediently followed the Lord in spite of what anyone else thought.

   chosing not to gossip when all the other girls at PE were. Dealing with peers in the chat room.

2. How does the example of Mary, the mother of Jesus, give us a model for the lifestyle of reckless abandon that God ordained for our daughters to walk in?

   she didn't question God, she faithfully obeyed even if she didn't understand, regardless of consiquences.

DAILY PRAYER

Father, I know You have incredible plans and dreams for my daughter. You have things ordained for her that can only be accomplished by Your mighty hand working in and through her life. I pray right now that You would strengthen her with the obedience and reckless abandon of Mary. You found her fit to give birth to Jesus, and Lord, I pray that you would entrust my daughter with giving "birth" to Your plans and purposes on earth. Help her silence voices of opposition and compromise that try to distract her from Your plans.

 And Lord, give me wisdom to see how You are moving and working in her life so that I don't become a voice that discourages her from following You.

In Jesus' Name, Amen.

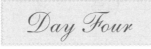

THE SECRET OF THE ALABASTER BOX

Read: *RALIW* Chapter 1, pages 38-41 (Read
Secret of the Alabaster Box section.)

This sinner had her dreams, and she wisely broke

her alabaster box in the presence of the only One

who can make a woman's dreams come true.

DAILY REFLECTION QUESTIONS

1. Read Luke 7:36-50. When you read about this sinful woman who broke such a valuable possession over the feet of Jesus, what does this act say to you about being a woman of reckless abandon?

_____

_____

_____

_____

2. Think about your daughter in this way. Has she already broken her alabaster box at the feet of someone not worthy of what's inside? Or is it sealed shut, awaiting the man worthy of the box's precious contents?

So far she has sealed it shut.

Note: This is not necessarily in regard to sexual purity, but rather your daughter opening up her life, her hopes, and her dreams to someone who did not regard those things as precious and costly, and ultimately treated them as worthless.

3. How can you encourage your daughter to give her dreams to God, entrusting them to Him *alone*?

Supporting her to have God as #1 in her life. to live counter-culturally. openly discuss life + who is a part of it

DAILY PRAYER

Father, help me show my daughter how precious her dreams are, that they are not worthy of being poured out before anyone— especially someone who would not value them. Protect her, Lord. Protect her from those who would treat all of the treasures You have put in her life as worthless.

In Jesus' Name, Amen.

RAISING DAUGHTERS WHO LISTEN TO THEIR HEAVENLY PAPA

Read: *RALIW* Chapter 1, pages 42-43 (Read *Raising Daughters Who Listen to Their Heavenly Papa* section.)

---

*O*ur daughters' trained capacity to hear and obey God
will profoundly impact their journey on planet Earth
and help them to discover God's best for their lives.

DAILY REFLECTION QUESTIONS

1. In view of the story about Gerta and her boots, why is instant and complete obedience to God so important?

   It Saved her life

   _____

   _____

   _____

2. On a scale of 1 to 10, how would you rate your level of swift obedience to God? Be honest. This is such an important area for you to be mindful of in your life because while your daughter may be listening to what you say, even more so she *is watching what you do!*

   | 1 | 2 | 3 | 4 | 5 | 6 | 7 | 8 | 9 | 10 |

3.   How do you model *swift obedience* to your heavenly Papa?

I do hope I am being a godly role model. I desire to live this kind of life

4.   How has your obedience caught the attention of your daughter?

I think so

DAILY PRAYER

You are Lord and Master. May my life be an example of someone who obeys You swiftly and completely.

More than listening to my words or even doing a Bible study with me, (Daughter's Name) is looking at my example. Empower me, Lord, to be a model of consistent obedience to You. Even when I fail and miss it, Holy Spirit, use that as a teachable moment that pushes her toward a lifestyle of instant obedience to a trustworthy Father.

In Jesus' Name, Amen.

BASIC INSTRUCTIONS FROM PAPA

1. Love the Lord your God with all your heart, soul, and mind (see Matt. 22:37).

2. Love your neighbor as yourself (see Matt. 22:39).

3. Make the Kingdom of God your primary concern (see Matt. 6:33).

4. Be anxious for nothing (see Phil. 4:6).

5. Pray without ceasing (see 1 Thess. 5:17).

6. Be a student of the Word (see 2 Tim. 2:15).

7. In everything give thanks (see 1 Thess. 5:18).

8. Forgive as freely as you have been forgiven by Christ (see Eph. 4:32).

9. Esteem others more important than yourself (see Phil. 2:3-4).

10. Say "Yes" to God's script rather than clinging to your own agenda (see Luke 1:37-38).

MOTHER/DAUGHTER SESSION

INSTRUCTIONS

You have both gone through Week 2 in the workbook (which covered Chapter 1 in the book). The focus of this week was your relationship with God. Here are some of the questions you can discuss during your mother-daughter session.

Ask *each other* these honest questions:

- Why is it so important to immediately obey God's voice?

- Has God ever told you to do something, and you hesitated? What happened?

- What does reckless abandon to God look like?

- Who are some people you know who would fit the description "recklessly abandoned to God" (both alive today, and back in the Bible times)?

- What are some of the benefits of being abandoned to God?

- Mom and Daughter—share testimonies of times you both have obeyed God instantly and watched Him do incredible things in your lives.

- What are some ways that you *both* can grow in your personal relationship with God?

This exercise is not about making anyone feel unspiritual or bad about their relationship with God. The wonderful thing is the Father is calling all of us deeper. All of us need to step up our level of reckless abandon, and as we do we will see God "step up" the blessing in our lives.

RAISING A YOUNG
LADY OF DILIGENCE

A holy hug, some encouraging words, an open heart and home, a willingness to serve, and a heart bent toward our Lord in prayer—these are worthy exercises to practice and to build into our daughters' lives. These are the actions and the fruits every mom can foster in her Young Lady of Diligence.

HUMILITY AND DILIGENCE: QUALIFICATIONS OF A WORLD-CHANGER

Read: *RALIW* Chapter 2, pages 45-47 (Read
Ruth's Diligence and *Humility and Diligence:
Qualifications of a World-Changer* sections.)

*D*iligence fortifies a person with the capacity to
continue long after everyone else has quit, either because
the task was too hard or not satisfying enough.

DAILY REFLECTION QUESTIONS

1. How does the story of Ruth and her work ethic model diligence to
us as mothers and daughters?

She was working hard for some one
elses benefit. She was other
oriented not self interested

2. Why is diligence such an important attribute to develop in a young
lady in waiting?

It is a quality that takes time,
intention it is a humble quality.
It is being like Jesus.

3. List some areas in your daughter's life that are examples of diligence. Celebrate them! Likewise, what are some areas she needs to develop further?

* Playing piano.
* youth activities.
This is an area that doesn't come naturally for Alyssa. She needs to make a conscience effort.

DAILY PRAYER

Lord, thank You for what is available on the other side of diligence. Accomplishment. Character. Endurance. Perseverance. Thank You for developing these characteristics in my life and in my daughter's life.

Reveal the areas in my life that have not been given to diligence. Holy Spirit, empower me to confront these areas, and, by Your grace, make the necessary changes. This will not only benefit my life, but it will model diligence to my daughter and encourage her to make the necessary changes as well.

In Jesus' Name, Amen.

DILIGENCE AND INTERNAL JOGGING

Read: *RALIW* Chapter 2, pages 47-48 (Read *Diligence
and Internal Jogging* section.) The remainder of this week,
we are going to focus on some essential characteristics
of a Young Lady of Diligence. On some days, we will
go through two to three topics. Today, we are starting
with and focusing on one of most essential—prayer.

---

*T*he prayer life of a Young Lady of Diligence can be
life-impacting from a very young age. As with physical
exercise, the only way to fail at prayer is to fail to show up.

DAILY REFLECTION QUESTIONS

1. How does the phrase "internal jogging" relate to your prayer life?

   *You have to develop it. It does
   not just come naturally.*

2. How can you model to your daughter a prayer life where everything
   is "on the table" and she is encouraged to pray about anything?

   *monkey see   monkey do!
   take notice of God daily, be thankful,
   be grateful, confess
   1 Thess. 5:17 pray continually*

3. Do you currently experience this type of openness and freedom with God in your prayer life? If not, *why not?*

yes, I have developed my prayer life. It is important to ~~be~~ have open communication with God

4. Based on First Thessalonians 5:17, what does it mean to "pray continually"? How can you model a lifestyle of continuous prayer to your daughter?

Praise God always in everything

DAILY PRAYER

Father, I pray for a free and open prayer life where You and I talk about everything and anything. Nothing is off limits and everything is something we can talk about. Show me how to model this kind of prayer before my daughter. Change the way she may think about prayer. If she sees it as boring, dull, and just another spiritual chore, help me to model something that is full of life, power, and passion.

In Jesus Name, Amen.

A HOLY HIT LIST AND PRAYING FOR HER CRUSHES

Read: *RALIW* Chapter 2, page 49 (Read *A Holy Hit List* and *Diligent Prayer for Her "Crushes"* sections.)

Teaching our daughters to pray for those who need Jesus is a most holy habit.

DAILY REFLECTION QUESTIONS

1. What does it mean to make a "holy hit list"? Have you ever done something like this before? (Maybe using a different name?) If so, what results did you see?

   change in my heart, change in my attitude, change in my life, change in the person's I was praying for. Some times took decades

   When you think your daughter is "crushing" on a certain boy, then pray for him and ask her to pray for him. Such prayers are a wonderful "heart guard" for daughter and mom!

2. List some benefits of diligently praying for the boys whom your daughter is "crushing on."

Safe-guard my heart + my
daughters through prayer

3. How can praying for these boys position God to speak to your daughter about her "crushes"? What might He tell her?

She is seeking God's best,
His path, direction, protection
from heart break

DAILY PRAYER

Thank You, Lord, that prayer is not just preparation for a great work—it is the greatest work! Show us the importance of making a list of those who need Jesus. Help us to diligently pray for their salvations—and celebrate when they come to know You! Give us names to put on this list and words to pray over their lives as the Holy Spirit is working.

And Lord, when there is a boy whom my daughter likes— help me not to just write it off or respond incorrectly. Help us, together, to diligently pray for his needs, family, and any specific situations going on in his life, as well as seeking Your will on this relationship.

In Jesus' Name, Amen.

HOLY SWEAT AND PIGGY BANKS

Read: *RALIW* Chapter 2, pages 50-52 (Read *Diligence and Holy
Sweat* and *Diligence and Breaking One's Piggy Bank* sections.)

*W*orking up a holy sweat of service is an offering
to God—a "sweat offering" that will come back as
a blessing upon a young person's own heart.

DAILY REFLECTION QUESTIONS

1. How does your daughter engage in "holy sweat" in her life?
    (Examples: household chores, church services, community involve-
    ment, etc.)

    I think Alyssa is pretty good.
    I can see God at work in this
    area. She seems better in some areas
    of service than others.

2. How can you help re-shape your daughter's view of service by show-
    ing it to be a blessing and not a curse? (Read Proverbs 31:10-31 for
    some pointers.)

    pray, encourage, model, mentor
    allow God to re-shape

Nothing is more touching than to see a young person give of her limited funds to a needy cause—whether in church, school, or community.

3. How can you encourage your daughter to be unselfish in giving to the needs of others, particularly those who are less fortunate?

live it! Snow them how people are less fortuniate than us.

4. How can you model this behavior to your daughter? (See Proverbs 31:20.)

community volunteer

DAILY PRAYER

Father, show me how to model a life of service and selflessness before my daughter. I pray that my life would be an invitation for (Daughter's Name), that she would pursue making an investment in others' lives through service and her funds. Holy Spirit, search my life for those areas that need to model diligent service and selflessness more. Enable me to walk this walk, so that my daughter would see these words in action.

In Jesus' Name, Amen.

HALLMARK CARDS, JUNK-FOOD DRAWERS, AND HOLY HUGS

Read: *RALIW* Chapter 2, pages 52-57 (Read *Diligence and Hallmark Cards, Diligence and a Junk-Food Drawer,* and *Diligence and Holy Hugs* sections.)

*W*hether e-mailing, texting, or even writing a card,

God's girls can keep hope alive in the hearts of those

they love—simply by being cheerleaders of truth!

DAILY REFLECTION QUESTIONS

1. How do you model being an encouragement to others—in front of your daughter? Is this something that comes naturally to her, or does she need some guidance?

walking along side people who are struggling. getting involved in the mess of life

Your daughter will want to invite friends into her home precisely because she has grown up watching her mother extend such hospitality to friends and (hopefully) to some strangers.

2. How would you currently rate your hospitality? How can you create a culture of hospitality in your home that impacts your daughter?

we host weekly Bible Study

A good hug is a gift to the human heart. It doesn't require special training, a college degree, or a bank account. Yet the benefits are priceless.

3. Are you prone to hug people, or are you a more hands-off type of person? How would the simple act of hugging people model love and kindness to your daughter (and encourage her to do likewise)?

I will hug when needed.

DAILY PRAYER

Lord, I invite You to fill my heart with kindness, genuine love, and concern toward people. Let this love so shine before my daughter that she would be encouraged to express Your love toward those who need it in real, physical ways—words of encouragement, hospitality, or a loving embrace.
In Jesus' Name, Amen.

MOTHER/DAUGHTER SESSION

INSTRUCTIONS

You have both gone through Week 3 in the workbook (which covered Chapter 2 in the book). The focus of this week was diligence. Here are some of the questions you can discuss during your mother-daughter session.

1. What does "diligence" mean to the *both of you*?

   hard work.

2. How does being diligent impact the following areas of life?

   - Prayer life

   - Relationships

   - Work

   - Serving other people

3. Are there areas in your lives where you can say, "Yes, I am diligent," or "No, I need some help on being diligent with that"?

4. What do you think the benefits of being diligent are?

5. For example, what happens when you are diligent in the following situations?

- Diligent to pray for the guys you like (daughter).

- Diligent to encourage your friends and family members.

- Diligent to serve others (in church, community, etc.)

- Diligent to use your money to help other people.

6.   Based on First Thessalonians 5:17, what does it look like to be diligent in prayer?

One of the greatest ways we can practice diligence is through prayer. Paul tells us to pray *continually* or *without ceasing* (see 1 Thess. 5:17). Take this time to pray about specific needs or people whom you want to commit to diligently pray for. Write their names down somewhere visible where you can constantly be reminded to pray for them.

As you watch God move in these situations and people, it is so important to track the progress, write it down, and then celebrate it together. Focusing on testimonies of God's faithfulness in answering prayer (that you participated in!) actually strengthens our diligence.

— Sierra
— Rian
— Rhylie
—

RAISING A YOUNG LADY OF FAITH

*Y*ou and your daughter can make a difference in this world through the daily growing of your faith in our incomparable God. Just because a girl is too young to date doesn't mean it's too early to train her heart toward the Lover of her Soul.

GETTING HER SEVEN DAILY

Read: *RALIW* Chapter 3, pages 59-63 (Read
Ruth's Faith, Getting Her "Seven" Daily, and *Do
I Need to Repeat Myself? Yes!* Sections.)

I took the instruction to "get my seven" very seriously,
and actually couldn't wait to read my Bible. From that day
until this day, I have never "recovered" from this privilege.

DAILY REFLECTION QUESTIONS

1. Why is it so important for you to spend daily time in the Scriptures?

   It is our blue print for daily
   life. If we are not in the
   word we won't be living according
   to it

2. How does reading God's Word—*even if it's just for seven minutes a
   day*—build and strengthen your faith? (See Romans 10:17.)

   We hear the word and grow
   it impacts how we live our
   lives what we do, or don't
   do. The word shapes + molds
   our thoughts + attitudes and
   comes out through our actions

3. In what ways do you "repeat" the Word of God to your daughter/
    children, communicating its truths to her/them on a regular basis?
    Why is it important for you to constantly be sharing Scripture with
    them? (See Deuteronomy 6:5-7.)

    - life style. we live reflects God
    consistantly
    - church attendance
    youth group
    bible study   personal devotions

DAILY PRAYER

*Lord, stir my heart to love Your Word even more than I do now.
Show me ways to constantly keep its truths in front of my eyes
and in front of my daughter. Help me to set an example of faith
for her as I commit to spending time in the Scriptures daily—
even if it's only for seven minutes.*

Thank You for the power and promises contained in its pages.

In Jesus' Name, Amen.

NO-BOZO HEART GUARD

Read: *RALIW* Chapter 3, pages 63-64 (Read
A No-Bozo Heart Guard section.)

*Y*our consistency is an invaluable model. The challenges
you are facing in life require strong faith, and faith is
inextricably linked to one's daily "face time" with God.

DAILY REFLECTION QUESTIONS

1. What practical results has studying God's Word produced in your life?

   I am more confident in making good decisions, I am gaining godly wisdom + guidance in every aspect of life

2. How can constantly feeding her heart on the Word of God set your daughter up to *avoid* making bad relationship decisions?

   She will be seeking God's best. Her "godly radar" will be tuned in to God's Spirit direction + purpose

3. What are some ways you can encourage your daughter to pursue God's Word—even if it's just for seven minutes a day? (One of the keys is sharing testimony with your daughter of *how* God's Word has produced results in your life. If you are currently not experiencing these results, it is time for you to *get your seven* and start watching God do incredible things in *your* life.)

- model, pray, encourage her to be in the word

DAILY PRAYER

Lord, I pray that You would stir (Daughter's Name) to hunger for Your Word. Also, help my relationship with You be an example and model to her. If there are things that need changing in my life, reveal them to me and help me change. There is no condemnation. You're not angry or upset with me. You are simply inviting me to experience depths of You that I have not experienced before. Thank You, Lord, for all there is available in Your Word. Open my eyes, and open my daughter's eyes to the riches contained in its pages, and stir us to hunger for everything You want to share with us.

In Jesus' Name, Amen.

OVERCOMING THE
DISTRACTION OF BUSYNESS

Read: *RALIW* Chapter 3, pages 65-67 (Read
Too Busy to "Get Your Seven" section.)

If you think you are too busy to read the

Bible, I promise you, you aren't.

DAILY REFLECTION QUESTIONS

1. Why do you feel too busy to read the Bible? Even if you have incorporated regular Bible reading time into your lifestyle, have you ever felt this way? If so, why? (This is important, as young people constantly feel like they don't have time.)

    priorities, laziness, distance from God, something else has taken 1st place.

2. How have you benefitted from "quiet time" with God in the Scriptures? Think of some specific examples of times you have enjoyed rich fellowship with the Lord in His Word. What made these times so enjoyable? (These are the benefits you need to share with your daughter.)

-answers to pray
- God's direction, purpose, guidance
- closeness with God

3. Does your daughter have a regular quiet time with God? If not, what are some ways you can model this to her? (Again, this is not something you can force her to do, but when she sees how you benefit from time with God, she will start to desire it.)

I have tried to encourage Alyssa so often. I have had to release her to God as it will become a nagging resentment if I force the issue

DAILY PRAYER

Father, I ask for wisdom on how to show my daughter the benefits and blessing of spending time with You—in Your Presence and in Your Word. Increase the richness of our time together, that I would grow hungrier for the wonderful truths contained in Your Word. Also, show me some practical strategies on how to help (Daughter's Name) spend time with You and reap the benefit of a deep relationship with You.

In Jesus' Name, Amen.

help Lord Jesus connect the mind + the heart. give her the desire to be in your word.

YOU CAN'T SMUDGE HIM OUT

Read: *RALIW* Chapter 3, pages 67-71 (Read
Ruth and a Kidnapped Girl—Two Hearts of Faith
and *You Can't Smudge Him Out* sections.)

I have told so many people that God can use them even
during their darkest hours when their faith has been outrun
by their pain and bitterness has crept into their hearts!

DAILY REFLECTION QUESTIONS

1. Read Ruth 1:16. How did Ruth's faith motivate her to leave behind her old life (and old gods) and follow the God of Israel? How would this faith ultimately lead her to meeting Boaz?

   She trusted the God of Israel.
   regardless of the bleak circumstances

2. Read Second Kings 5:1-4. How did faith in God protect the young Israelite girl (who was kidnapped) from letting bitterness and unforgiveness define her?

   she knew He was able to heal,
   save + protect regardless of where
   she was

71

3.   How can God still use you, even in your darkest hours? Can you recall some instances where, in spite of bitterness, anger, unforgiveness, or pain, God still used you to minister to someone? (These are key characteristics to model before your daughter, for they reveal the extent to which God loves and powerfully uses His children, broken though they may be.)

To be a light or example to those who are watching both believers and unbelievers

DAILY PRAYER

God, thank You for using broken people. Thank You for using me! For all of those times when I didn't have it together, or when I was dealing with pain, anger, frustration, unforgiveness, bitterness—all of that—thank You that Your light continues to shine through the darkness, revealing Your goodness to someone in need. And God, in many cases, that someone has been me. I also know that "someone" is my daughter. Reveal Yourself, Lord, to her through my life—even in the darkness. Show her Your power and unfailing love as You reveal Your nature, Your purposes, and Your joy through broken people.

In Jesus' Name, Amen.

KEYS TO CULTIVATING FAITH THROUGH STUDYING THE WORD

Read: *RALIW* Chapter 3, pages 71-74 (Read *Q.T. Kiss Method for You and Your Daughter, Jesus Calling, Red Circle of Trust, One Year Bible Method,* and *Incomparable Benefit of Bible Reading: Growing Faith* sections.)

*J*ust because a girl is too young to date doesn't mean it's too early to train her heart toward the Lover of her Soul.

DAILY REFLECTION QUESTIONS

1. Which of the Bible study options that Jackie presented sound most appealing to you? If you are already on a Bible study program, which one are you currently using and what benefits have you been experiencing as a result?

   journaling. → multi sensory always helps Ocement things into the mind. internalize it.

2. How will developing habits of spending time in the Word actually strengthen your daughter's faith? How will this impact the decisions she makes and sustain her through difficulty?

- cultivating godly habits/disciplines.
- word of God will be hidden in her heart
- word of God comes to mind when needed

3. Specifically, how will your daughter's growing and maturing faith sustain her as she ventures out into the relationship world? (As you write down these benefits, remember, you as mom get to invest into your daughter's growing faith.)

It is training her heart towards Jesus.
Jesus is first place everything else follows.

DAILY PRAYER

Father, I thank You for the growing, maturing faith that time in Your Word develops. Again, show me how to help (Daughter's Name) pursue Your Word in a deeper way. Help me to avoid making it sound religious or like some type of obligation. In fact, show me how to clearly share the benefits and joy and peace and power and wisdom that come from being connected to Your Word. Take (Daughter's Name), Lord, and develop her into a woman of strong faith—faith that sustains her through every storm and every situation of life, keeping her anchored in Your Truth, Your love, and Your unending faithfulness.

In Jesus' Name, Amen.

KEYS TO EFFECTIVE
BIBLE STUDY

Practical preparation for your quiet time:

- The same chair

- The same Bible

- The same journal (journal in composition book, journal book, or the Bible margins)

- A notepad

- The same pen

- Study helps nearby—*ESV Study Bible* for the hard questions

WHAT IS AVAILABLE DAILY IN GOD'S WORD?

(From Psalm 119)

- Wonderful truths (see verse 18)

- Wise advice (see verse 24)

- Encouragement for the discouraged (see verse 25)

- Hope for those in grief and despair (see verse 28)

- Discernment between worthy and worthless things (see verse 37)

- Wisdom beyond one's years (see verses 99-100)

- Insight to spot false belief systems (see verses 104,130)

- Rest and peace for the weary soul (see verse 165)

MOTHER/DAUGHTER SESSION

INSTRUCTIONS

You have both gone through Week 4 in the workbook (which covered Chapter 3 in the book). The focus of this week was faith. Here are some of the questions you can discuss during your mother-daughter session:

- What are the benefits to spending time in God's Word?

- When the phrase "spending time with God" is used, what comes to your mind? Is it boring and dull? Is it sitting in a room, reading a book?

- If you have a negative impression of what "spending time with God" looks like, in what ways can you start changing the way you interact with God?

- How does spending time in God's Word build up your faith?

- How does spending time in God's Word cause you to avoid making bad decisions?

- In what ways have you both experienced God's Word actually protecting you from making a bad choice?

- Do you feel like you have time to read the Bible? Are you both too busy? If so, how could you arrange your schedules to spend more time in God's Word?

- What are some ways that would help you read the Bible more often? What do you think about the "Seven Daily" program? Is this a method that would help both of you *stay* in the Word more consistently?

I would like both of you to commit to this: Take the next seven weeks (for the remainder of this study) and spend at least *seven minutes* in God's Word each day. Don't try to push for more or settle for less.

I know you're busy. God knows you're busy! That said, I really pray that, after reading this chapter on raising (and becoming) a young lady of faith, you see the benefit of spending time with God—in His Word and Presence.

RAISING A YOUNG LADY OF VIRTUE

The leading man in the Book of Ruth was drawn to the leading lady because of the obvious virtue displayed in her life through her choices. In modern times like these, virtue is not what most guys are concerned about; they are often too busy looking at the exterior and are not even concerned about the interior.

WHAT DOES VIRTUE LOOK LIKE?

Read: *RALIW* Chapter 4, pages 77-81 (Read
Ruth's Virtue, Is Virtue Extinct in the 21st Century,
and *You Are More Than Your Breast Size.*)

A woman of virtue is irresistible to a godly

man. Virtue is a pearl worth pursuing.

DAILY REFLECTION QUESTIONS

1. What is your understanding of virtue? How does Ruth model this
   virtue in Ruth 2:10-11, thus making herself attractive to Boaz?

   The character of the inner person.
   - loyal, faithful, integrity, hard work,
   godly, pure,

2. As a mom, how can you help your daughter develop virtuous qualities in her life that do *not* attract the wrong type of guys?

   talking to her, instilling godly
   values, modelling it.
   living life together

3. How much do you pay attention to what your daughter wears and how she presents herself? How does what she wears communicate a message to guys (who are looking)?

A lot we talk about it every time we get clothes.

DAILY PRAYER

Father, help me instill the blessing and reward of a virtuous character in my daughter. Give me eyes to see what she is wearing, how she is presenting herself to the world, and what image she is projecting.

Help me to lovingly show (Daughter's Name) her value so that she feels no need to reveal herself in the wrong ways in front of the wrong people.

Above all, help me to show her the value that You have placed on her as Your daughter. May her understanding of value protect her and keep her walking in virtue.

In Jesus' Name, Amen.

WHY MODESTY?

Read: *RALIW* Chapter 4, pages 81-83 (Read *Help with Modesty for Moms* and *Modesty and Little Girls* sections.)

*D*oes your daughter have a consecrated closet?
Does she dress modestly, or is she eye candy for
the boys as well as the men around her?

DAILY REFLECTION QUESTIONS

1. What does the following quote say to you about modesty: *"Modesty is presenting yourself so that the attention of other people is drawn to your face"*?

   what we wear matters. We have
   a choice on how others view us,
   by what we wear

2. How can/do you model modesty to your daughter?

   - not wearing low fitting tight clothes.
   - talk about it in movies, around
   town. in our home

3. Read First Corinthians 6:19-20. How does recognizing that we are temples of the Holy Spirit change the way we think about modesty?

true beauty comes from within. to display godliness internally our external should be a reflection of that.

DAILY PRAYER

Father, I pray you would continue to show (Daughter's Name) that as a believer, she is a temple of the Holy Spirit. Your Holy Presence lives inside of her. She has been saved to not only go to Heaven one day, but to represent Jesus on the earth.

Show her what she carries and what she offers the world as a daughter filled with the Presence of King Jesus. The more she realizes who You are, the more she will present herself modestly. Help me to model this to her as well. Modesty is not being unfashionable—it's reflecting the beauty and holiness of what's on the inside. May (Daughter's name) be so aware of her identity as Your daughter, and one who carries the Presence of the Holy Spirit, that she pursues modesty instead of just tolerating it as the Christian thing to do.

In Jesus' Name, Amen.

WHO SHE DATES REFLECTS WHO SHE IS

Read: *RALIW* Chapter 4, pages 83-86 (Read *Who Do Young Ladies of Virtue Date?* and *Toothpicks in Eyeballs* sections.)

$\mathcal{D}$ating is not simply a social activity. Who your daughter wants to date is a reflection of her depth, spiritually speaking. You need to pay attention to which boys your daughter is crushing on, because it reveals her heart.

DAILY REFLECTION QUESTIONS

1. Based on Second Corinthians 6:14, why is it important that Christians date other believers? (Even if it is only just "one date.")

   every date is a potential mate. do not be yoked with unbelievers

2. How can dating a believer (who is *actually* passionate for the Lord Jesus Christ and not just "Christian" in title only) set a young woman up for the future?

   They are on the same path moving together towards similar goals

3. How do the guys your daughter wants to date reflect her spiritual depth? Why is it important that you pay attention to the kinds of guys she wants to date?

The deeper the spiritual growth the more likely they will be looking / attracting guys who are spiritually mature as well.

DAILY PRAYER

Lord, help me be aware of the types of guys (Daughter's name) wants to date. Show me what this reveals about where she is in her relationship with You.

If she is pursuing the wrong guys, Lord, help her to see her value and not compromise by dating someone who does not know You or who is not serious about You.

Above all, may her relationship with You be the most important thing in her life. May that be the ultimate value and trait she looks for in a potential boyfriend—someone who shares her ultimate passion, Jesus.

In His Name, Amen.

THE GREAT SELF-DECEPTION

Read: *RALIW* Chapter 4, pages 86-88 (Read
Greatest Self-Deception—Missionary Dating and
Even Ninth-Grade Boys Know This sections.)

A common self-deception among girls as well as women
is the power that the girl thinks she has to change the one
she has a crush on, admires from afar, or has begun to date.

DAILY REFLECTION QUESTIONS

1. How is it deceiving for our daughters to think that they can change
    the guys they have crushes on—believing that they can lead these
    guys into a relationship with Jesus by dating them?

    we can not change anyone.
    only God can make true
    lasting changes. + that is only
    if the person wants it.

2. In what ways is a believer who dates a non-believer blatantly dis-
    obeying the clear commands of the Lord? (See 2 Corinthians 6:14.)

    Do not be un-equally yoked
    is a very clear passage.

3. Why is it self-deception to think you can change another person's behavior? Have you ever experienced this? If so, how can you use what you have learned to help protect your daughter from doing the same?

I tried changing your dad in the early years. It only led to fighting / Frustration. Thankfully I realized this + surrendered him to God.

DAILY PRAYER

Lord, protect (Daughter's Name) from believing the lie that she can change a guy. Only You change hearts, Holy Spirit.

Show (Daughter's Name) that the best thing she could possibly do is wait for someone who believes the same things that she does and upholds the same values that she does. If these beliefs and values need to be enforced or strengthened, help me to constantly be investing in shaping these in our home and in her life so that she actually desires to date someone who passionately loves Jesus and who doesn't just wear the label, "Christian."

In Jesus' Name, Amen.

PRAY FOR A "TIGGER" IN YOUR DAUGHTER'S LIFE

Read: *RALIW* Chapter 4, pages 89-91 (Read the *Pray for a "Tigger" in Your Daughter's Life* section.)

---

*M*oms, just as you want to pay attention to the boys your daughter pays attention to, so you want to be aware of the friends she surrounds herself with. Parents teach virtue, but friends enhance or tarnish virtue.

DAILY REFLECTION QUESTIONS

1. Does your daughter have a friend, peer, or slightly older mentor in her life who is encouraging her spiritually? If so, who? If not, this is a relationship you want to start praying for. (Like "Tigger" was for my daughter, Jessi.)

_____

_____

_____

_____

2. Why is it important for you to pay attention to the friends your daughter surrounds herself with? Are her friends positive influences on her life? Do they build her up? Do they encourage her spiritually?

You become like the people you hang out with. (yes)

3. What does your daughter see modeled in your life with the friends and company you keep? Does she see you with people who propel you closer to God, or does she see you socializing with women who are spiritually mediocre and do not encourage your walk with Jesus?

I have great friends/models

DAILY PRAYER

Lord, thank You for what you are doing in (Daughter's Name)'s life! I ask that you would continue to bring her friends who build her up spiritually and strengthen her faith. I pray you would sur-round her with people who are authentically on fire for Jesus; He is their passion and desire! Real people who pursue a real God. Not religious people, Lord. Not legalists. Not those who poorly represent Jesus. Lord, my prayer is that You alone would be her joy and reward. May the friends in her life push her toward this pursuit!

In Jesus' Name, Amen.

VIRTUES CHECKLIST

(Not exhaustive, but a good start!)

a. Courage (see Josh. 1:6-8)

b. Honesty (see Isa. 33:15; Ps.15:2)

c. Respect (see Prov. 9:10; Eph. 6:5-9)

d. Generosity (see Prov. 11:24)

e. Compassion (see Eph. 4:32; 1 Pet. 3:8)

f. Patience (see Ps. 37:7-9)

g. Perseverance (see Rom. 5:3-5)

h. Loyalty (see Prov. 17:17)

i. Forgiveness (see Matt. 18:21-22)

MOTHER/DAUGHTER SESSION

INSTRUCTIONS

You have both gone through Week 5 in the workbook (which covered Chapter 4 in the book). The focus of this week was virtue. Here are some of the questions you can discuss during your mother-daughter session:

- What does the word "virtue" mean to you?

- How does what you wear and how you present yourself communicate virtue?

- In what ways does *virtue* attract the right guys? (Remember how Ruth attracted Boaz through her virtue? He was the right guy.)

- How has the concept of "modesty" been explained or portrayed to you? What do you think of when you think of someone who is "modest"?

- What does it mean to be *a temple of the Holy Spirit*, and how should this impact the way we present ourselves (see 1 Cor. 6:19-20)?

- How can you pursue modesty instead of just tolerate it as the "Christian thing to do"? (It's amazing the knock that modesty has taken in the media, especially because of the outspoken Christians who have endeavored to uphold morality and godly values.)

- Why is it so important to date other believers?

- What does the following statement mean? "The guys you date reveal your spiritual depth." How does that work?

- *Missionary dating*—what does this mean to you, and why is it a terrible idea that sets us up for disappointment?

- Do you have spiritual mentors in your life? If so, who are they and how has their influence been a help to you and your relationship with God?

It is so important for us to have the right people in our lives, encouraging us to press on toward all of the things God has in store for us. Virtue is fueled by the virtuous influencers in our lives. Do your friends build you up spiritually? Do you have crazy faith friends like the guy in Mark 2, whose friends were so full of faith and trust in Jesus that they lowered the paralyzed guy down through the roof? Talk about faith-*full* friends!

Week 6

RAISING A YOUNG LADY
OF DEVOTION

*R*aising a daughter to be a Young Lady of Devotion
who seeks to know God's heart is the very best investment
you can make to ensure that she will safely attract a
man who also has a connection with God's heart.

RELENTLESS DEVOTION TO JESUS

Read: *RALIW* Chapter 5, pages 93-95 (Read *Ruth's Devotion* and *Modeling Hope or Hopelessness* sections.)

*O*ur devotion to God is primarily about our relationship with Him, and certainly our passion for Him, but those we love are watching that devotion as it ebbs and flows through our lives each day.

DAILY REFLECTION QUESTIONS

1. How does our view of God determine our level of devotion to Him? For example, if we believe God is "cold and exacting," angry, and constantly upset with us, how will we respond to Him? How will we respond differently if we see Him as a loving Father who offers an unending flow of grace, mercy, and acceptance?

   The view/thoughts/feelings we have towards God directly impacts how we interact/the depth of our relationship with God

2. Does your daughter see you model hope or hopelessness? How do you usually respond to God in the midst of a trial, circumstance, or challenge? What does this reveal about your devotion? (This is not

intended to make you feel bad, but rather to strengthen your devotion if it tends to wane in the midst of difficulty!)

They see me as I am. I dont hide things from them. I try to model the real deal.

3. Why is it important for your devotion to be constant? What does this say about your relationship with the Lord, and what model does it present to your daughter?

unchanging, unwaivering the same yesterday, today, tomorrow. is how God models to me. I want to be in His image.

DAILY PRAYER

Lord, help me to be a carrier and releaser of hope. If I tend to be more hopeless and downcast, fill me with Your joy.

If my relationship with You changes and shifts based on the season I am going through or the situation I am dealing with, take me to the next level of maturity. May I be a woman of constant devotion to Jesus so that my daughter would have a strong example to follow.

In Jesus' Name, Amen.

MOM ON A MISSION

Read: *RALIW* Chapter 5, pages: 95-98 (Read
Unfathomable Impact of a Devoted Mom and
Mission Fields at the Front Door sections.)

You and I will someday give an accounting
for the spiritual influence we had not only on
our children but also all the other children who
came into our lives through our children.

DAILY REFLECTION QUESTIONS

1. In what ways are you a spiritual leader in your household? Do you
    share the responsibility with a husband who is committed to Jesus,
    or are you the one responsible for the family's spiritual atmosphere?

    -I am responsible for the spiritual
    atmosphere. Christian education,
    devotions, prayer
    Jason does youth group. we do
    church as a family.

2. How does your husband's devotion to Jesus encourage the family's
    spiritual growth?

3. As a mom, you are one of God's greatest secret weapons! What does this mean to you when it comes to your role as a "missionary" to your daughter's friends? Are there friends she has right now in whom the Lord is encouraging you to make an investment of love and encouragement?

Jenna (chair)
Rhonda (boss)

PRAYER FOR MOTHER AND DAUGHTER

Father, help me embrace the calling to be a missionary in my home. Empower me to create an atmosphere where You receive great glory and where You are given the opportunity to do great works—both in my family and in the lives of everyone who comes through those doors.

May I take this assignment seriously. As people come into my home, help me to invest time, Your love, encouragement, an openness to listen, and whatever else they need into their lives.

In Jesus' Name, Amen.

THE PRAYER INVESTMENT

Read: *RALIW* Chapter 5, pages 98-101 (Read
Prayer Requests in a Photo Album section.)

---

*F*riends can be the best kind of cheerleaders for each
others' spiritual growth, but they can also tease and
undermine each others' spiritual lives. Devotion to
Jesus has a differentiating impact on whether or not our
daughters will be Bozo magnets or Boaz magnets.

DAILY REFLECTION QUESTIONS

1. What ways do you pray for your daughter's friends? If this is
something you have not started doing yet, what ways can you start
praying for her friends? (These are some of the people she is around
most, who influence her the strongest. If you are praying for them,
you are spiritually directing the course of your daughter's life and
positioning her friends for salvation and increased devotion to Jesus).

I go through cycles of
praying for their friends.
It is important

2.   Can you name at least one of your daughter's girlfriends who she feels at liberty to talk about spiritual things with? Do her girlfriends show spiritual growth you can see, or is it in title or talk only?

_____

_____

_____

_____

3.   How do you and your friends engage in edifying conversation about the Lord? Are the spiritual conversations you have with your friends a reflection of what you would like your daughter to share with her girlfriends?

I have a lot of edifying conversations with many Christian ladies.

PRAYER FOR MOTHER AND DAUGHTER

Lord, thank You for the gift of prayer. Remind me daily to invest prayer into (Daughter's Name)'s friends. Help me to call them out by name before Your throne, and pray Your perfect will over their lives. Give me ears to hear what You are saying—if there are specific things You want me to be praying about for them. Above all, I pray Jesus would be their passion, that they would burn for Him and Him alone.

In Jesus' Name, Amen.

DELIVER US FROM THE KINGDOM OF SELF

Read: *RALIW* Chapter 5, pages 101-105 (Read
*Deliver Us From the Kingdom of Self, Rescue Me from
Me,* and *Mom: The Original Drug Dealer.*)

---

*M*e-centric living is in the heart of every

man and woman, boy and girl; but it is either

enhanced or diminished by those who love them,

beginning with those who raise them.

DAILY REFLECTION QUESTIONS

1. How is "self" one of our greatest enemies as believers? In what ways is "self" glorified in the world, influencing the next generation through culture, media, entertainment, et cetera?

   we are focussed internally. we are not
   looking at how selfishness affects others.
   The world makes it look good, they
   "sell" the me, me, me, industry

2. What does the phrase, "Rescue Me *from* Me" mean to you? How can you rescue your daughter from living a "me-centric" lifestyle? (And

prevent yourself from becoming your child's *drug dealer?*) What are some ways you can show your daughter it is not *all about her?*

helping her take the focus off herself. by giving, serving, doing for others with no personal motive. not over indulging or giving into tantrums.

3. Why is it absolutely important for you to be comfortable saying *no* to your daughter?

She won't have self control and will become disastisfied with things/people. It produces a shallow character.

DAILY PRAYER

Father, deliver me from the trap of self-centeredness. I know it impacts all of us. Show me areas in my life where I am addicted to self and ovation and praise. Thank You, Holy Spirit, for the power to walk in victory over self. Even though I am stuck with self as long as I live on the earth, I am also filled with Your Spirit for all of my days. He alone gives me power over self and enables me to focus on Jesus and His Kingdom work.

In a world that is becoming more and more self-centered, help my daughter to keep her eyes fixed on Jesus. May she be captivated by His beauty and glory, so much so that the temptation to be distracted by self-centeredness is not even appealing to her!

In Jesus' Name, Amen.

This is a weak area. right now. for both Alyssa and me. I am not doing a good job. Lord help me

TWO ENEMIES OF DEVOTION: ENTITLEMENT AND GLORY ROBBERS

Read: *RALIW* Chapter 5, pages 105-108 (Read
Entitlement Trumps Gratitude and *Glory Robber*
Versus the Lady of Devotion sections.)

The Young Lady of Devotion knows how to bring
glory to God and not rob Him of such glory! May we,
by God's grace, raise daughters who are not "ovation-
aholics" but God-glorifying Young Ladies of Devotion.

DAILY REFLECTION QUESTIONS

1. What does it look like to be a "glory robber"? How does this work it-
   self out practically in our everyday lives?

   _____

   _____

   _____

2. Does your daughter spend more time focusing on me-centric things
   (everything is all about *her*), or does she express genuine passion for

Jesus, concern for others, and a desire to move past the popularity of being me-centered? What are some of the tell-tale signs of either one (being me-centric or God/other-centric)?

_____

_____

_____

_____

3. Would you describe yourself as a lady devoted to Jesus or more of a people-pleasing "ovation-aholic"? (Be honest. Again, God reveals things that He wants to transform and heal!) How has your daughter modeled your behavior?

_____

_____

_____

_____

DAILY PRAYER

Father, may Your glory and ovation be my top pursuits. There are so many opportunities for me to take credit for something, to go after recognition, or seek affirmation when the most important thing in my life is giving You the glory due Your name. Without You, I am nothing and can do nothing.

Develop this attitude in my life so I can model it for my daughter. Help me to be a woman devoted to Jesus. Set me free of any tendencies to pursue ovation or acclaim that would deprive me of the wonderful opportunity of giving Jesus all of the glory!

In Jesus' Name, Amen.

Together

MOTHER/DAUGHTER SESSION

You have both gone through Week 6 in the workbook (which covered Chapter 5 in the book). The focus of this week was devotion. Here are some of the questions you can discuss during your mother-daughter session:

- Why is it so important to keep constant in our relationship with God? How does this reveal true devotion to Him?

- What does our relationship with God project to the people watching us? (In other words, what does it reveal about our devotion to Him when we are up one day, down the next, and all over the place the rest of the time?)

- Who are some people that you can think of who model steadfast devotion to Jesus?

- Why is it so important to wait for a man who is a spiritual leader—completely devoted to Jesus, not simply wearing the Christian name badge?

- Who are some people you could be praying for (friends)?

- What kinds of conversations do you have about God with your friends? Are they edifying and faith-building?

- What does it mean to be "set free from self"? How is "self" a major enemy when it comes to our devotion to God?

- How is saying "No" actually a good thing?

- What does an "ovation-aholic" look like?

God is not looking for or expecting perfection from you. This is why He gave us Jesus! However, even though we do miss it, blow it, and make mistakes, in the midst of it all we can be wholly devoted to Jesus. Even in our sin, how we respond reveals our devotion to our Master. The world needs to see Christians who are serious. Not wishy-washy. Not all over the place. Devotion is revealed by steadfast commitment. These are the types of people a lady of devotion should surround herself with, from the friends you spend time with, to the guys you date. Ask yourself: Are they pushing you toward steadfast commitment to Jesus, or are they encouraging you to compromise?

RAISING A YOUNG LADY OF PURITY

A woman's purity is, in fact, a lifelong guard of her heart.

RAISING A LADY IN WAITING...
IN A SEX-SATURATED SOCIETY

Read: *RALIW* Chapter 6, pages 109-111 (Read
Ruth's Purity and *Sex-Saturated Society* sections.)

Just as Ruth's purity allowed her to go to Boaz,
request that he function as her kinsman redeemer,
and exit his presence as pure as she entered, our
girls can sustain purity even in a context that
greatly challenges their commitment to purity.

DAILY REFLECTION QUESTIONS

1. Why do you think there is this idea that it is *impossible* to raise pure girls in a sex-saturated society? Why does it seem like such a daunting task?

   "everyone is doing it" Fighting
   an uphill battle. media, t.v., celebrities
   make sexuality enticing

2. What are some of the obstacles that you perceive your daughter deals with in pursuing and maintaining purity in a sex-saturated culture?

Alyssa has a good handle on this.

3. How does purity guard your heart?

guards it from temptation. Physically, spiritually, mentally, emotionally.

DAILY PRAYER

Father, I know the world is saturated with impurity. Our culture is absolutely consumed with it. Even though it seems like a difficult task to raise a daughter who pursues purity, I believe that by Your grace, and using Your wisdom, it is possible.

In fact, Lord, I ask You to help me raise up a daughter who shines Your light in the midst of darkness. May her life testify to the benefit of going after purity. Not because Mom says to, or a pastor tells her to, or because she is "guilted" into it. I pray she would be one who pursues purity because she desires purity. Show (Daughter's Name) the blessing that purity plays in actually protecting and guarding her heart.

In Jesus' Name, Amen.

THE PRINCIPLE OF DIMINISHING RETURNS

Read: *RALIW* Chapter 6, pages 111-114 (Read *MPDP* =
Mandatory Pre-Dating Prep, The Law of Diminishing Returns, and
The Law of Diminishing Returns: Sexual Brinkmanship sections)

---

*G*od made the human body sexually for a particular

progression—one that is meant to be followed to its

end in the context of marriage. So that very chemistry

He wired us with is designed to yearn for more.

DAILY REFLECTION QUESTIONS

1. After reading this section, write out your understanding of what the
    Law of Diminishing Returns is:

    One thing leads downhill quickly
    to the next. It seems to
    start with an innocent hand
    hold before you know it you went
    too far

2. When you read the *Natural Progression Toward Sexual Sin* section on
    page 112, are there aspects of it that seem surprising?

    no

---

3. Why is it so important to encourage your daughter to set up strong physical boundaries (so that the *Natural Progression Toward Sexual Sin* you read about does not take place in her life)?

It is a life long guarding/protecting of purity, even after you are married

DAILY PRAYER

Father, help (Daughter's Name) form strong, healthy boundaries in her life. As we go through this study together, I pray she would understand that her body is Your temple and that it is both deserving and demanding of the greatest respect. Show her that even though everyone else may be "doing it," compromise and going "too far" actually devalue her in the sight of the guys she likes.

Again Lord, I pray that You would show (Daughter's Name) the value You place on her. As she understands her identity and worth, may she reject anything or anyone who would invite her to go down a path of compromise.

In Jesus' Name, Amen.

ALWAYS PUSHING THE LIMITS

Read: *RALIW* Chapter 6, pages 114-119 (Read *Striving
for the Chemistry High, Quicker Sexual Brink in the Next
Relationship, Drawing the Line: Remember the No Zone,*
and *Why Do Christian Kids Go Too Far?* Sections.)

*W*hat your daughter doesn't know is that
with physical touch she is always progressing
toward a more potent physical thrill.

DAILY REFLECTION QUESTIONS

1. How does one physical touch progress toward a more *potent* physical
    thrill (if there are no clear boundaries preventing this progression)?

    we were designed to want more.
    There is a chemical reaction
    going on inside of us.

2. How does going to the "No Zone" set the stage for sex?

    we become blinded by
    our intoxication. and
    cant see, think, act clearly

3. How do you see yourself explaining these principles to your daughter and instructing her in some of these more uncomfortable topics? Does the notion of sharing these things with your daughter make you feel embarrassed? If so, evaluate the options: Would you rather experience brief embarrassment or sit back and idly watch your daughter make decisions that could have disastrous effects on her life and future?

we are very open and freely talk.

DAILY PRAYER

Lord, empower me to boldly share these principles with my daughter. Help me not to preach to her or come off in some "know-it-all," condemning way. God, I ask that You help me to direct her in love. Help her to see it. Even if it feels embarrassing and uncomfortable—I don't care. She means more to me than my feelings do.

Holy Spirit, empower me to press past how I feel for a moment, or even a brief season, so that I can honestly invest in (Daughter's Name). I know the payoff will be worth it all!

In Jesus' Name, Amen.

THE COST OF GOING TOO FAR

Read: *RALIW* Chapter 6, pages 119-122 (Read *Sex Ruins
a Good Relationship, Treat Your Girlfriend as a Younger
Sister,* and *Additional Encouragement to Wait* sections.)

---

*T*he painful reality is that most young people grow up
hearing that sex before marriage is not God's design
without ever hearing about the high price of premarital sex.

DAILY REFLECTION QUESTIONS

1. How does sex ruin a good relationship *or* create a bad one? Have you seen this happen in any of your daughter's friends? In other people you may know? What have been some of the results of premarital sex in their relationships?

   it recks the friendship. I have seen this happen.
   bondage, brokeness, abortion, pregnancy jail

2. Read First Timothy 5:2. How can you explain this concept of "treating a girlfriend like your sister" as something that is not *gross*, but instead something that will honor her and treat her with the respect that she deserves?

not doing anything with a sister in Christ that you would not do with a blood sister. that means not getting physical at all!

3. Based on the list provided on page 121, what are some of the consequences of premarital sex (beyond just the damage it does to a relationship)? These are the consequences you need to coach your daughter to avoid by pursuing purity.

Suspicion, guilt, fear communication break down respect / loss of trust deception, · post-marital insecurity unfair comparisons.

DAILY PRAYER

Lord, protect my daughter from the consequences of premarital sex by leading her to pursue purity. I come to You again, Lord, praying for (Daughter's Name) that she would go after purity because she wants to. If she spends her time simply trying to resist having sex or going "too far" in her own strength, she will grow tired. It will become overwhelming.

Empower (Daughter's Name) to really become passionate about purity because of what it does for her and says about her. As a result, I thank You that she will avoid Bozos, and all the junk and sexual expectations they bring with them.

In Jesus' Name, Amen.

NEVER TOO YOUNG...

Read: *RALIW* Chapter 6, pages 122-125 (Read *Never Too Young to Learn About Waiting, Judging Promiscuous Girls Prematurely Robbed of Purity*, and *21st Century Sodom and Gomorrah* sections.)

---

*T*he driving reason I write books like this and speak to and with thousands of women each year is to encourage, exhort, and beg all of us in the Body of Christ to heed this particular call from God to come out and be separate.

DAILY REFLECTION QUESTIONS

1. How did you respond to the story of Nancy Claire and her Valentine's gift from the little boy? Did you think Nancy's mom was too extreme in how she responded? Regardless of your current feelings on the story, in the context of purity, how was Nancy's mom setting her daughter up for success down the road?

   Not allowing her to get sucked into superficial flattery. that would led her away from godliness

2. Why is it very important to instill these values of purity in our daughters—when they are still *very young*?

set boundaries, foundations, install values, ~~rooting~~ them in truth so they don't stumble. giving tools + equipping her for success.

3. What are some of the factors that make a girl promiscuous? How does God want us to respond to girls who have been caught in this trap? Are any of your daughter's friends in this place now? If so, *don't judge them*; instead, *pray* for them! Write their names down on your prayer list or in this workbook and pray.

Emily

~~Bee~~ Lizzy

DAILY PRAYER

Lord, I see that this world is in a moral crisis. Instead of focusing on the problems and judging the people, help me to be part of bringing solutions. For every problem person I experience, for every promiscuous girl I hear about in my daughter's school, may I bring them to You in prayer. You are the solution, Jesus. Focusing on the problem makes it easy for me to judge. Help me to pray solutions. And Lord, help me to raise up a young lady of purity who is also part of being the solution in her generation.

In Jesus' Name, Amen.

MOTHER/DAUGHTER SESSION

INSTRUCTIONS

You have both gone through Week 7 in the workbook (which covered Chapter 6 in the book). The focus of this week was purity. Here are some of the questions you can discuss during your mother-daughter session:

- Why do people think that pursuing purity is impossible in our culture?

- What are some of the obstacles we face daily that try to discourage us from pursuing and maintaining our purity?

- *The Law of Diminishing Returns*—what does this mean to you,.and what did you think about it?

- Did the process seem surprising? Extreme? Or right on target?

- Why is it so important to establish clear boundaries *before* getting into a dating situation?

- How does what you do with your body expose how you perceive your value?

- Do you feel comfortable talking about the kind of stuff you read in this chapter, or is it embarrassing? If so, why do you feel like it is embarrassing? (To talk about it *and* to listen to it?)

- How have you been exposed to purity in the past? (Was it presented in a condemning way? Was it simply a "Don't have sex until you're married" lecture? Who did you hear share about it and how did it impact you?)

- How does becoming physical with a guy either destroy a good relationship or prolong a bad one?

- What did you think of the Nancy Claire Valentine's Day story? Was Mom being too extreme, or do you see the value she was communicating to her daughter?

- Why is it so important to pursue purity from a young age?

- How does your relationship with God encourage you to pursue a lifestyle of purity?

It begins with God and ends with purity. You have well-meaning people telling kids not to cross the line *every single day*. Result? They continue to reject purity. Purity is the result of everything we have read thus far. When we are devoted to Jesus and see the value *He* places on us, impurity doesn't even feel like an option anymore.

RAISING A YOUNG LADY OF SECURITY

*W*hatever people say about me, I accept; but I lay the comments alongside Jesus' biographical sketch of me, because that is where I live, rest, and have confidence.

MOM: THE MODEL OF SECURITY

Read: *RALIW* Chapter 7, pages 127-129 (Read *Ruth's Security* and *Daughters Reflect Your Security and Insecurities* sections.)

---

*G*rowing up, the most obvious model a daughter has is her mother. Moms can model the security they find in the Lord, as Ruth certainly did. We can also model "finding" insecurity in all kinds of things.

DAILY REFLECTION QUESTIONS

1. How do you deal with insecurity? As a mom, have you learned to take your insecurities to God and rest in Him, or do you try to deal with them yourself?

   I think I try to take them to God. I am filling myself with truth and don't walk in the worlds views. (magazines, movies etc.)

2. In what ways does your daughter model your security or insecurity? How does she deal with worry? Self-image? Confidence? More often than not, how daughters respond to these things is a reflection of the example they saw in Mom.

I think I model security and see that displayed in my daughter

3. Reflect on *your* childhood. How did your mother model insecurity/ security to you? Are any of these attributes seen in *your daughter*? If so, reflect on how you might be modeling some of the behavior you saw in your mother (good or bad).

by the grace of God I don't model most of my mom's attributes. Anger is one I do see though in both Alyssa + myself. we are both aware + trying to deal with it biblically

DAILY PRAYER

Lord, show me how to be an example of security that (Daughter's Name) can model in her own life.

Expose me to the insecurities that I have and continue to deal with. Reveal them so we can work through the healing and restoration process. Show me areas where my trust is not in You, but in shakable, unstable things.

Help me to place my complete trust in You—in Your love, in Your Word, in Your promises, and in Your plan. You will never let me down!

In Jesus' Name, Amen.

THE LOVE TANK DEFICIT

Read: *RALIW* Chapter 7, pages 129-133
(Read *Insecurity and a Love Tank Deficit* and
Oh God, Keep an Eye on Her sections.)

$\mathcal{G}$rowing in your understanding of the love
of God as Father will help fill your daughter's
love tank. This is important, because love tank
deficits are readily exploited by the enemy.

DAILY REFLECTION QUESTIONS

1. What does the "Love Tank" concept mean to you? Specifically, what does a deficit in this area produce in your daughter?

   like a gas tank you have to continuosly fill it so it doesn't become empty. In this senerio it produces bozo but

2. What are some factors that can contribute to a low "Love Tank" for your daughter?

   Not having her needs met by her daddy

3. Read John 17:11. How does the fact that *Jesus* Himself prayed for your daughter bring you comfort? How does this impact your prayers of protection over your daughter?

we as an indivioual matter.
I need to line my prayers
up with Jesus' prayers

DAILY PRAYER

Father, I come before You today with two specific prayers:
One—I ask you to fill my daughter's love tank. May she be satis-
fied in Christ and Him alone. May Jesus be her Rock and source
of security for the rest of her life.

Two—I come into agreement with the Prayer of Jesus in John
17:11. Thank You for releasing protection over (Daughter's
Name)'s life and for preserving her purity.

In Jesus' Name, Amen.

OVERCOMING THE ENEMY'S LIES

Read: *RALIW* Chapter 7, pages 132-136 (Read *Screaming the Truth* and *With God, Who Could Be Against Her* sections.)

The father of lies screams lies at our hearts
daily. We can only scream back if our hearts
are wallpapered with the truth.

DAILY REFLECTION QUESTIONS

1. What does it look like to "scream back" at the enemy in response to his lies?

    take your thoughts captive.
    to fight lies with the truth

2. The ability to "scream back" at the enemy and overcome his lies has everything to do with knowing *the truth*. Re-read the list I provided on page 134. Which of these truths do you struggle with? Which ones do you notice your daughter struggling with?

---

3. Why is being confident in the love of God and the love of her family so important for your daughter? How can increasing her security in these areas protect your daughter from sexual sin?

DAILY PRAYER

Father, increase (Daughter's Name)'s confidence in Your love and in the love of her family. May the love and acceptance she receives from You and from me help her to make the right choices.

Protect her from people and places that would try to influence her otherwise. Even though she cannot be shielded from them, I pray that she would reject anything that would push her to compromise her purity for security and acceptance.

In Jesus' Name, Amen.

READY TO DATE YET?

Read: *RALIW* Chapter 7, pages 136-139 (Read
Timeline for Dating and *The Gift of No* sections.)

---

*I*f your child cannot say no without worrying about
what her friends think—over a movie or music or
certain activities—then she is not ready to date. The
ability to say no is inextricably linked, not only to the
virtue of your child, but the security of your child.

DAILY REFLECTION QUESTIONS

1. What are some attributes that would make a girl *not ready* to date
    yet? How does her security and self-confidence factor into identify-
    ing an appropriate timeline for dating?

    _____

    _____

    _____

    _____

2. How does being able to say "no" in small things impact whether or
    not your daughter is able to date?

    _____

    _____

_____

_____

3. Why does insecurity attract older, predatory guys? Why does getting attention from older guys interest younger girls? Why is this a *major problem?*

_____

_____

_____

_____

DAILY PRAYER

Lord, strengthen (Daughter's Name) to say no. May she be quick to say it because of what she gets at home. May I never say "no" because I want to limit her or restrain her from enjoying life. I pray she would always understand that my "no" and the boundaries I set for her are to protect her. They are designed to work with You, Lord, and set her on a course toward the life You have designed for her.

Just like Your commandments are not burdensome and are for our good, I pray You would reveal to her how saying "no" protects her from potentially ruining her life. In the end, may it impact her deeply so that she is bold enough to say "no" to compromise, insecurity, and making bad decisions.

In Jesus' Name, Amen.

DEALING WITH BULLIES, MEAN GIRLS, AND BOZO BOYS

Read: *RALIW* Chapter 7, pages 139-143 (Read *Source of Insecurity for All Teen Girls*, *Secure Enough to Face Bullies and Mean Girls*, and *Forgiving Bozo Guys and Mean Girls* sections.)

*P*rayer can do what God can do. And it will

help your daughter see God as her defender—

with the co-defender of an attentive mother!

DAILY REFLECTION QUESTIONS

1. Review the list on pages 139-140. How many of these things are a struggle for you? (After all, our girls mirror *our* insecurities.)

_____

_____

_____

_____

2. In what ways has your daughter dealt with bullying or *mean girls*? How did she handle these interactions? What did you do to step in and help?

_____

_____

_____

_____

3. What are some appropriate ways for you (and your daughter) to re-
    spond to bullying, mean girls, or mocking Bozo boys? (Remember
    my letter to Kristi about Nancy Claire.)

_____

_____

_____

DAILY PRAYER

*Father, show me how to pray for the bullies and mean girls whom
my daughter has to deal with (or has had to deal with).*

*Dealing with people like this is a normal part of life. In the pro-
cess of it all, show us—both my daughter and I—how to release
these people to You in prayer and how to release their offense from
our lives with forgiveness.*

In Jesus' Name, Amen.

COMMON WORRIES FOR TEEN GIRLS

Here is a list that was the result of interviews with teen girls age twelve to fifteen. The girls were asked to share the things they worried about. This list is a reminder for all moms to pray for the development of a Young Lady of Security.

- Girls talking about me

- What other people think about whatever you're doing

- If my friends are really going to be my friends around other people

- If I get in a fight with my friends, are we going to hate each other and become rivals?

- Spiders

- Grades

- Boys

- Friend situation (who is being mean)

- Rumors

- Succeeding in school and in general

- Trying to be good at everything

- Trying to make myself worth someone's time

- Fighting with siblings

- Loneliness

- Screwing up my life and not realizing it

- That people will think I'm weird

- Not making the right choices

- Gaining weight

- If people judge me from my appearance

- That I won't know how to get out of a bad situation

- Getting into trouble

MOTHER/DAUGHTER SESSION

INSTRUCTIONS

You have both gone through Week 8 in the workbook (which covered Chapter 7 in the book). The focus of this week was security. Here are some of the questions you can discuss during your mother-daughter session:

- What are some ways people deal with insecurity?

- How do *you* deal with insecurity?

- What is our "love tank" and why is it so important to keep it full?

- What are some ways to keep this "love tank" full?

- Why is it important that we learn to "scream back" at the enemy and his lies? What does this mean to you?

- What are some of lies that the enemy tells you that cause you to become insecure? (These are the very things you need to "scream back" at.)

- Why is it is important for us to know the truth in order to deal with the lies of the enemy?

- Explain some of the factors that you think make a girl *ready* to start dating?

- How comfortable are you saying "No"?

- How is it a problem when older guys express interest in younger girls?

- What are some ways to handle bullying or "mean girls"?

I know it may seem a bit strange at first to "scream back" at the enemy. Of course, I'm not always meaning that you are supposed to yell at the top of your lungs at him. (Although there is a time and a place!)

The reality is that insecurity is the result of believing his lies. When we worry. When we question our value in God's sight. When we stumble over who we are or who we're not. When we think that having a boyfriend or getting in *that* relationship with *that* person will mean that "we've arrived"—we have fallen into the trap. This is where we need to scream, ladies. Our security is in Christ alone. He has given us value. The cross reveals the beyond-expensive value He has placed on us.

RAISING A YOUNG LADY
OF CONTENTMENT

"Wait."

Such an assignment is not given to cause suffering, but to prevent it. Women experience so much needless pain when they run ahead of God's format.

DISCONTENTMENT THAT SUFFOCATES JOY

Read: *RALIW* Chapter 8, pages 149-151 (Read *Ruth's Contentment* and *Discontentment Suffocates Joy* sections.)

*W*hen we find ourselves discontented, we are all too often focusing on what is missing from our lives rather than seeing what is going well with them.

DAILY REFLECTION QUESTIONS

1. How does being *boyfriend-less* produce discontentment in many girls? Why do you think this is such a big issue? (What factors make girls think that being in a relationship is being content?)

   When you focus on whats missing in your life rather than all the good things that are happening. Focussing inward rather than outward. Pity party. Poor me.

2. In what ways does comparison breed discontentment and ultimately steal our joy? How do you personally deal with comparison and discontentment?

   It makes you feel inferior like you are not good enough. don't look at magazines. celebraties.

3. How is self-pity *inverted* pride? What does it mean to have an "over-inflated view of what one deserves"?

addictive, gives temporary pleasure
seperates you from reality

DAILY PRAYER

Father, I thank You for all of the blessings You have given me. They are too many to count. I pray that instead of being caught up in comparison or discontentment, I would give myself to thankfulness. Even when I deal with the temptation to be discontented, empower me to lift my eyes and focus on who You are, what You've done, and what You are doing.

Create in (Daughter's Name) the same spirit of thanksgiving and gratitude. May this attitude be a weapon against the comparison, discontentment, and self-pity that is so popular and rampant in her generation.

In Jesus' Name, Amen.

SERVING OTHERS AND SILENCING THE WHINING

Read: *RALIW* Chapter 8, pages 151-157 (Read
Contentment and Holy Sweat, Contentment and Boredom,
and *Limit Self-Indulgent Emotionalism* sections.)

---

*L*earning contentment does not mean expecting

changes in our circumstances, but expecting

Jesus to be enough in our circumstances.

DAILY REFLECTION QUESTIONS

1. How does serving others (being a Young Lady of Diligence) develop your daughter into being a Young Lady of Contentment? How is serving other people a "perfect escort out of self-pity" and something that enhances contentment?

   <u>Proverbs 11:25 he who refreshes</u>
   <u>others will be refreshed himself</u>

2. In what ways can you encourage your daughter to serve others (as an alternative to being bored)? Start with this: What are some specific

ways your daughter has demonstrated service toward others in the past? What areas is she passionate about? Encourage her in these things! Cheerlead her to use her talents to be a blessing to someone else.

Philippians 4:11-13
art of contentment

3. How does whining and self-centeredness actually set girls up to attract Bozo guys? Evaluate your daughter. Is she content, or is she heard frequently whining? Evaluate the influences in her life: Who might be whining and bringing her along on their bandwagon? Stop to evaluate yourself as well. Remember, you're her top model!

me, me, me attracts others that
are self-centered
end is disaster.

DAILY PRAYER

Father, I want to help (Daughter's Name) grow in contentment. If there are areas in my own life where I display discontentment or model whining in front of my daughter, help me break free from this behavior. I receive Your empowering grace to do what I cannot do in my own strength and set a new standard for my daughter to follow.

In Jesus' Name, Amen.

DEALING WITH UNREALISTIC EXPECTATIONS

Read: *RALIW* Chapter 8, pages 157-160 (Read *Discontentment and Loneliness, Contentment and Unrealistic Expectations,* and *Want a "Ten" But Keep Getting a "Five"* sections.)

---

*W*hen your daughter has a dateless Friday night or even a "friendship dateless" one, it is for her a ready tutorial in contentment through the strength of Jesus.

DAILY REFLECTION QUESTIONS

1. How can we embrace loneliness as God's will *for right now* and accept it as a positive thing?

   It is our heart attitude, how we see things cup half empty or half full.

2. How can you use disappointing situations and circumstances as teachable moments in your daughter's life?

3. What is your understanding of the "Ten Versus Five Theory"? How can applying this perspective save both you *and* your daughter from experiencing disappointment and being constantly let down because of unrealistic expectations?

the "10 days" are high lights in our lives. They can't be on the everyday level. change your expectations to be more realistic. Save yourself from disappointment

DAILY PRAYER

Lord, may I set my expectations according to Your plans. I can't do it all, and I am not expected to! I understand that many people have expectations that they place on me. I also place expectations on myself. Help me to seriously evaluate what is most important so I can take care of those things and fulfill those obligations. Otherwise, I will do what I can, but I will not become disappointed because I can't do it all. That's real life!

In the same way, set (Daughter's Name) up so that she refuses the unrealistic expectations that the world, her friends, and even she places upon herself. Give her wisdom to evaluate what is most important and most realistic.

In Jesus' Name, Amen.

SOME KEYS TO DEFEATING DISCONTENTMENT

Read: *RALIW* Chapter 8, pages 161-165 (Read
*Discontentment Blinds Us, Boy Craziness: A Common Assault
on Contentment,* and *Cheering on Discontentment* sections.)

---

*C*ontentment does not flow from finally getting the

approval of others. Contentment flows from knowing

one has already been approved by the King of kings!

DAILY REFLECTION QUESTIONS

1. What are some areas in your life where you are dealing with jealousy toward those who have what you have always wanted? (These are your "Rachels.") How does jealousy actually enhance your discontentment and blind you to God's blessing in your life?

   you get tunnel vision. and focus on the wrong thing.

2. How does "boy-craziness" rob girls of contentment?

   It is not finding contentment/trusting God. It brings strife + heartache

147

3. In what ways do friends and peers actually *encourage* discontentment in our lives? How have you experienced this in the past (or present)? What advice could you share with your daughter when she experiences the same thing from friends/peers?

pushing you into "boycraziness"
hounding you
making you feel like there is something
wrong with you.

DAILY PRAYER

Father, remind me that my value and worth are in You. They are not in what other people have. Reveal areas of jealousy in my heart. I confess these to You now and receive Your forgiveness. (Take this time to search your heart and confess any jealousy to the Lord.)

I'm grateful to be forgiven, but I am also grateful to be empowered to help other people. Lord, show me how to raise a daughter who is not moved by what others have. I pray she would be so content with herself, and in the assignment You have given her, that nothing would distract her and pull her off-course.

In Jesus' Name, Amen.

LIST OF THE TOP TEN WAYS TO BUST BOY-CRAZINESS

1. Write love letters to God.

2. Create a list of great movies and books that don't fuel impure thoughts and romance.

3. Hang out with friends who aren't boy-crazy.

4. Invest time in the "man in your life"—your dad.

5. Exercise or get involved in sports.

6. Get a mentor to talk to about it.

7. Write a list of your future husband's qualities.

8. Begin a journal to your future husband.

9. Read *Passion and Purity* and *Lady in Waiting*.

10. Go on a mission trip.

STARVING DISCONTENTMENT AND FINDING A BIBLICAL MODEL

Read: *RALIW* Chapter 8, pages 165-168 (Read
"Don't Waste Brain Cells, Child," Don't Feed
Discontentment Through Toxic Giving, and *Ruth, the
Proverbs 31 Woman,* and *Contentment* sections.)

The next time you have to say no to a purchase for your

child or say no to arranging special opportunities for them,

just remember the propensity to "toxic giving" and how

it can ultimately poison a child with discontentment.

DAILY REFLECTION QUESTIONS

1.   What are some things in your life that help you "bust discontent-
     ment" (just like Ella's discontentment-buster list on pages 165-166)?

- not comparing my life to others
- not watching t.v. / commercials
- being focussed on eternal things
- trying to live a simple life

2. How can we feed discontentment through "toxic giving"? What does this look like and how does it create an attitude of entitlement in our children?

giving everything to them. not making them wait or earn it themselves

3. Think about creative ways you could use Ruth and Proverbs 31 to minister to both your daughter *and* her friends. Why are these portions of Scripture so important in raising young women who are content?

contentment starts with our thoughts and then our actions. It requires discipline + the renewing of the mind.

DAILY PRAYER

Lord, help me to steer my daughter away from discontentment in every way that I can. Let me starve it by not feeding "toxic giving." Give me wisdom on how to avoid creating attitudes of entitlement and dependency in her by giving her too much. Constantly keep me aware of the line between giving that blesses and demonstrates love and the toxic giving that will ultimately harm her.

Finally, show me how to live out the biblical model before (Daughter's Name) and teach her how to follow it as well. Give me wisdom to teach her, but above all the grace to live it so that any teaching or instruction I give is backed up by a lifestyle to prove it.

In Jesus' Name, Amen.

ELLA'S
DISCONTENTMENT-BUSTER LIST

(from pages 165-166)

- Never allow yourself to complain about anything—not even the weather.

- Never picture yourself in any other circumstances or someplace else.

- Never compare your lot with another's. (See Psalms 16.)

- Never allow yourself to wish this or that had been otherwise.

- Never dwell on tomorrow—remember that (tomorrow) is God's, not ours.

PARALLELS BETWEEN THE PROVERBS 31 WOMAN AND RUTH

I encourage you to find a way to use the following Scriptures as tools for a Bible study with your daughter—and if possible, some of your daughter's friends.

Perhaps over the course of eight weeks, as a group you can go through each of these characteristics, with each week being a different characteristic. Have your daughter/the girls look up these verses in their Bibles and talk about what they mean, how they apply today, and some ways they could incorporate them into their own lives.

1. Devoted to her family (see Ruth 1:15-18; Prov. 31:10-12,23)

2. Delighted in her work (see Ruth 2:2; Prov. 31:13)

3. Diligent in her labor (see Ruth 2:7,17,23; Prov. 31:14-22,24,27)

4. Dedicated to godly speech (see Ruth 2:10,13; Prov. 31:26)

5. Dependent on God (see Ruth 2:12; Prov. 31:30)

6. Dressed with care (see Ruth 3:3; Prov. 31:22,25)

7. Discreet with men (see Ruth 3:6-13; Prov. 31:11-12,23)

8. Delivered blessings (Ruth 4:14-15; Prov. 31:28-29,31)

MOTHER/DAUGHTER SESSION

INSTRUCTIONS

You have both gone through Week 9 in the workbook (which covered Chapter 8 in the book). The focus of this week was contentment. Here are some of the questions you can discuss during your mother-daughter session:

- How does being without a boyfriend make many girls discontent?

- In what ways do comparison and jealousy make us discontent with what we already have?

- Why does service to other people help develop contentment? (Especially to those who are less fortunate.)

- How does self-centeredness actually attract Bozo guys?

- What are some of the benefits of being alone?

- Why do you think so many people consider being alone such a bad thing? Do you think this has anything to do with how they understand their value? (Other people assign their value.)

- What does the "Ten Versus Five" theory mean to you?

- In what ways do people set themselves up for disappointment and discontentment through their own expectations?

- List some of the ways that our friends can actually discourage contentment.

- What does it mean to be content in the assignment that God has uniquely given to you?

- Explain the concept of "toxic giving" and how that *easily* creates discontentment in our lives.

Discontentment sets us up for poor decision-making. Why? We see what others have and either 1) think that is what we *need* when in fact, it is *not at all* or 2) even if it is a positive thing and we could benefit from it, we still become jealous of what they have and become willing to do all sorts of ridiculous things to get it— *now.*

Let's become okay with where we are and what we have *now.* I'm convinced that those who learn how to enjoy their *now* are being set up for an incredible *later.*

RAISING A YOUNG LADY OF CONVICTION

It is conviction in the principles of godly standards for dating and marriage that enables us to say "no" when that's required and to say "yes" to God's ways.

THE STARTING PLACE
OF CONVICTION

Read: *RALIW* Chapter 9, pages 171-175
(Read *Ruth's Convictions*, *A Lady of Clear
Convictions*, and *The Stud Purse* sections.)

*O*nce your daughter begins noticing the boys in her world,
it is time to develop the standards that define her convictions.

DAILY REFLECTION QUESTIONS

1. What is the "double booked" reality of the heart? How does this relate to the choices that we make daily? Why is it so important that your daughter is aware of this heart condition when it comes to dating?

   Keeping options open.
   make sure your heart and
   head are in the same
   place

2. How is developing her conviction the *most important* preparation your daughter can make before dating?

   It helps maintain a stand
   when tempted

_____

_____

3.   Identify some ways you can help your daughter distinguish between a Bozo and a Boaz. They are listed on the next page of your workbook.

_____

_____

_____

DAILY PRAYER

God, may I help my daughter prepare for dating in the best way possible. Beyond clothes, make-up, hair, and all of those external things, use me to help her develop deep convictions. This is something only Your Spirit can do, so I pray He would use me as an instrument.

Before I work with my daughter, help me to solidify my own convictions. For the areas where I have compromised and messed up and missed it, I thank You for grace. I thank You for forgiveness and second chances…and third chances…that Your grace is unending. I receive it. I reject the lie of the enemy that says, "You are unworthy to help your daughter develop convictions when you've compromised yourself." Jesus, You have set me free and I am free indeed. I am free to move forward and help (Daughter's Name) build strong convictions that will position her for Your best!

In Jesus' Name, Amen.

COMPARISONS BETWEEN A BOZO AND A BOAZ

(See Second Samuel 13 and Ruth 2.)

1. Bozo is controlled by emotion.

   - Boaz controls his emotions. (He may get upset, but knows what to do with it.)

2. Bozo is angered when he doesn't get his way.

   - Boaz can rise above disappointment; he knows God will give him peace.

3. Bozo doesn't notice the needs of others. (He might turn it on for you, but don't be impressed unless he does the same for the person across the table.)

   - Boaz is courteous and aware, goes the extra mile, and has plenty of room to love lots of people.

4. Bozo is very critical of others and very intolerant.

   - Boaz is tolerant of imperfection because he knows who he is.

5. Bozo is self-centered; he always wants it on his terms (lust thrives in this heart).

   - Boaz is other-centered, and therefore self-controlled (lust is constrained in his heart).

6. Bozo is rigid and his viewpoint is the only conclusion.

    ▪ Boaz is teachable; his heart and mind are open.

7. Bozo always makes excuses for not doing a task well. (If you marry a man like that, you become part of the excuse team.) No one is ever accountable for the way he lives and he always wants sympathy.

    ▪ Boaz strives to do his work to the best of his ability and to the glory of Jesus.

8. Bozo lacks integrity; he has no conscience when exploiting a girl's purity.

    ▪ Boaz has integrity and is kind, merciful, and gentle. These qualities fuel his protection of a girl's purity.

YOUR DAUGHTER IS CALLED TO BE A STANDARD-SETTER

Read: *RALIW* Chapter 9, pages 175-177 (Read *No Bozo Pajamas* and *Mentored by Hollywood* sections.)

---

*B*oys as well as girls are being babysat and
even mentored by Hollywood. This is how
they are learning about the opposite sex.

DAILY REFLECTION QUESTIONS

1. How is a generation being raised and mentored by Hollywood? What values are being instilled into our sons and daughters through the media?

   immediate gratification
   selfishness
   low standards

2. What are the advantages to raising a young lady of conviction who acts like a princess in God's Kingdom? Specifically—what does such an example reveal to the Bozo guys out there (who are unfortunately increasing in number)?

raise the bar
show them they can be
a gentle man.
you are worth it.

3. How do the convictions of young women in this generation actually set a standard for how the boys end up behaving toward them? (This is revealed in how these young women dress, present themselves, guard their purity, etc.)

Guys will respect you.
they will not try crap with you.

DAILY PRAYER

Thank You, Father, for the honor of raising up a daughter whom You have called to be a standard-setter in her generation. Make her aware of how her convictions actually play a part in how our young men are raised. Help her to see herself as valuable and treat herself that way.

I pray that as she protects her value through her convictions, boys will respect her and protect these things as well.

In Jesus' Name, Amen.

ESSENTIAL BOAZ QUALITIES

Read: *RALIW* Chapter 9, pages 177-180 (Read
Most Significant List on an iPhone section.)

*Y*oung girls need to decide in advance what a man
worth waiting for is like. You don't decide in the
moment when you're crushing on a guy. You decide
in advance—before the emotional tsunami hits.

DAILY REFLECTION QUESTIONS

1. What are some advantages to your daughter keeping a list of "ideal guy" traits always handy? How does continually focusing on this list actually set your daughter up to reject anyone less than her desired standard?

   It is there as a reminder
   of waiting for God's best

2. Why is it important for your daughter to create this list *before* she starts dating or "crushing on" someone?

   So that it is not compromised

3. How does a young lady of conviction actually remind guys of what they are supposed to act like?

they see a proper example of how to treat a girl.

DAILY PRAYER

Lord, help my daughter to create a list of the essential, non-negotiable qualities for her ideal guy. This doesn't mean he will be perfect. This doesn't mean he will be something out a fairy tale. We all come with issues and all are working through stuff. But show her the balance. And Lord, help me to pray for this man as well. (You might want to pray through the sample list provided on the next page.)

I pray that the he is a man radically committed to Jesus Christ—not in title or name only. I pray that she would pursue one who pursues and relies completely upon You. Help her to create this list as soon as possible. And Lord, show me how I can help and guide her through the process.

In Jesus' Name, Amen.

SAMPLE "MR. RIGHT" LIST

1. Spirit-controlled Christian

2. Jesus #1 in his life, not just an ornament

3. Broken: understands how to rely totally upon Jesus

4. Ministry-minded: wherever he is, he is available

5. Motivator: a man of vision, concerned about lost souls

6. Sensitive spirit: in tune to the needs of others

7. Understands the awesome responsibility of a husband to his wife

8. Humble enough to be a disciple (teachable) and able to disciple others

9. Man of prayer: knows the key to success is his private time with God

10. Family man: desires to have children and raise them properly for God's glory

APPEARANCES CAN BE DECEIVING

Read: *RALIW* Chapter 9, pages 180-184 (Read
Superficiality of Appearance section.)

*W*henever I hear girls describing guys as being so
cute or so hot, I always ask, "What is his heart like?
How does he treat those around him?" God's Word
speaks loudly to the superficiality of appearance.

DAILY REFLECTION QUESTIONS

1. How can physical appearances be deceiving? Can you think of some instances where you ended up dating someone strictly based on appearance, and, in the end, you wish you wouldn't have dated the guy *at all*?

2. Most likely, your daughter has certain physical preferences when it comes to the "ideal guy." How can you help her be open and flexible on some of the physical stuff to accommodate the more important things (namely, those qualities that *should* be on her "ideal guy" list)?

If the list is made up of mostly physical characteristics, there is some work that needs to be done!

_____

_____

_____

_____

3. What does the following statement mean: "Guys play at love to have sex?" How is this a warning to girls about the selfish, external intentions Bozo guys have when it comes down to sex and getting a girl to go "all the way"?

_____

_____

_____

_____

DAILY PRAYER

*Lord, help me to instill in my daughter the value of not being appearance-focused when it comes to dating. I pray that when it comes to those essential, non-negotiable characteristics of an "ideal guy," she always choose a godly character over someone she thinks is "hot" or "cute." Mature her, Lord. If she doesn't already, help her to see that external things are fading. Also show her that You are a good Father. You are the giver of good gifts, and You are not—**not** going to disappoint her when it comes to providing her with the ideal guy.*

In Jesus' Name, Amen.

Day Five

FIRE WALL OF PRAYER AROUND OUR GIRLS

Read: *RALIW* Chapter 9, pages 184-186 (Read
Fire Wall of Prayer Around Our Girls section.)

Your girls are around boys at church who are
Christians, but they don't live up to their names,
either. They are indeed princes related to the King
of kings, but they bring dishonor to that name.

DAILY REFLECTION QUESTIONS

1. How can you pray for the guys who show interest in dating your
    daughter—especially Christian guys who may not be *walking
    the walk*?

    _____

    _____

    _____

    _____

2. What is a pretty reliable way of determining whether a girl has been
    involved physically with her boyfriend?

    _____

    _____

3. In what ways are you going to commit to praying for your daughter *daily*? List *four* specific things you are going to pray over your daughter on a daily basis.

a. _____

b. _____

c. _____

d. _____

DAILY PRAYER

Thank You, Lord, for giving me the privilege and weapon of prayer. Even though I cannot be with (Daughter's Name) all the time, Holy Spirit, You are with her. As Jesus said, You are with her and You live inside of her.

I pray, first of all, that You would strengthen her convictions. Wherever she is, I know she can be stronger. We all can be. Lord, may her convictions be strengthened as she pursues a relationship with You above everything else. I pray nothing else this world offers would entice or allure her more than You. Show her the shallowness in all of the competition out there. Show her how lifeless and joyless it all is compared to knowing You.

In Jesus' Name, Amen.

FOR ADDITIONAL STUDY...

Women are well acquainted with the "ideal woman" chapter, Proverbs 31. Very few know about the "ideal man" chapter excerpted verse by verse, below.

Ruth 2:1-16

1. Now Naomi had a relative on her husband's side, from the clan of Elimelech, a man of standing, whose name was Boaz.

2. And Ruth the Moabitess said to Naomi, "Let me go to the fields and pick up the leftover grain behind anyone in whose eyes I find favor." Naomi said to her, "Go ahead, my daughter."

3. So she went out and began to glean in the fields behind the harvesters. As it turned out, she found herself working in a field belonging to Boaz, who was from the clan of Elimelech.

4. Just then Boaz arrived from Bethlehem and greeted the harvesters, "The Lord be with you!" "The Lord bless you!" they called back.

5. Boaz asked the foreman of his harvesters, "Whose young woman is that?"

6. The foreman replied, "She is the Moabitess who came back from Moab with Naomi.

7. "She said, 'Please let me glean and gather among the sheaves behind the harvesters.' She went into the field and has worked steadily from morning till now, except for a short rest in the shelter."

8. *So Boaz said to Ruth, "My daughter, listen to me. Don't go and glean in another field and don't go away from here. Stay here with my servant girls.*

9. *"Watch the field where the men are harvesting, and follow along after the girls. I have told the men not to touch you. And whenever you are thirsty, go and get a drink from the water jars the men have filled."*

10. *At this, she bowed down with her face to the ground. She exclaimed, "Why have I found such favor in your eyes that you notice me—a foreigner?"*

11. *Boaz replied, "I've been told all about what you have done for your mother-in-law since the death of your husband—how you left your father and mother and your homeland and came to live with a people you did not know before.*

12. *"May the Lord repay you for what you have done. May you be richly rewarded by the Lord, the God of Israel, under whose wings you have come to take refuge."*

13. *"May I continue to find favor in your eyes, my lord," she said. "You have given me comfort and have spoken kindly to your servant—though I do not have the standing of one of your servant girls."*

14. *At mealtime Boaz said to her, "Come over here. Have some bread and dip it in the wine vinegar." When she sat down with the harvesters, he offered her some roasted grain. She ate all she wanted and had some left over.*

15. *As she got up to glean, Boaz gave orders to his men, "Even if she gathers among the sheaves, don't embarrass her.*

16. "Rather, pull out some stalks for her from the bundles and leave them for her to pick up, and don't rebuke her."

After studying this chapter, consider reading the contrasting "Bozo" chapter: Second Samuel 13:1-16.

Together

MOTHER/DAUGHTER SESSION

INSTRUCTIONS

You have both gone through Week 10 in the workbook (which covered Chapter 9 in the book). The focus of this week was conviction. Here are some of the questions you can discuss during your mother-daughter session:

- How does clearly defining your convictions prepare you for relationships?

- Discuss the list of characteristics comparing a Boaz and a Bozo.

- In what ways is a generation being raised and mentored by people in Hollywood?

- How does a woman of conviction actually have the ability to set the standards for men in society?

- Explain how creating a list of "ideal guy" traits (and keeping it *very handy!*) is so important to maintaining your convictions.

- What type of emphasis do people place on physical appearance when it comes to being attracted to someone and dating them? How important is appearance?

- How can physical appearances be deceiving, and ultimately very destructive to a relationship?

Earlier on, we talked about how you cannot change a guy by dating him, thus the insanity of *missionary dating*. That said, I believe that as a generation of young women rise up who model deep convictions (one such conviction being the refusal to date someone who does not share her deep convictions), the moral temperature has to change. Bozos will start seeing that their tactics and tricks are failing because a new kind of woman is arising.

I believe the young lady in waiting is part of a movement that will change the way women are viewed entirely. Your convictions don't just protect you, but they are modeling what conviction looks like to the many eyes that are watching.

RAISING A YOUNG LADY OF PATIENCE

*M*y heart's passion is twofold: for all of God's girls to wait for His best; and for me to be used as His instrument to encourage their waiting, whether it be for a husband and family, a vocation, or any other calling of God.

ENTERING THE SCHOOL
OF PATIENCE

Read: *RALIW* Chapter 10, pages 191-198

(Read *Ruth's Patience, Is "Wait" a Cuss Word,* and

Vulnerability to Missionary Dating sections.)

---

*T*eaching our children how to postpone present

pleasures for future fulfillment is a concept that is familiar

to most of us. Yet it is less frequently practiced in our

more recent "fast food," "instant access" generations.

DAILY REFLECTION QUESTIONS

1. What do our children learn when we teach them how to *postpone*
    present pleasures for future fulfillment? How does patience shape
    their character and specifically prepare our daughters for their Boaz?

    Waiting for things develops
    Character
    waiting is a prerequisite
    for God's best.

2. How do you model patience to your daughter? (Remember, your home life is the apprenticeship for either patience or impatience, selflessness or selfishness.)

I need improvement ★ *I am especially not patient at meal time.*
→ *delayed gratification for trips; or big items. is modelled.*

3. Why do you think so many young girls are so negative toward the idea of *waiting* for God's best?

they have been trained to get everything right Now! instant gratification generation

4. How does impatience actually set a girl up to become vulnerable to "missionary dating?"

not waiting for God's best in His timing, lowering the bar.

DAILY PRAYER

Lord, I ask that You reveal areas in my life where I am not being patient. I know we all blow it sometimes. But God, I want to at least model a consistent attitude and character of patience before my daughter. I pray our home is that place of apprenticeship where she not only learns the principles of patience, but she actually understands its value.

In Jesus' Name, Amen.

DON'T SETTLE

I hope you don't consider me to meddle,
When I say don't settle.
Have you heard my heart scream?
Don't give up your dream.
So many have settled for Prince Harming,
Rather than courageously wait for Prince Charming.
Settling for a Bozo,
Whose heart will be a no show.
Despairing over your absent knight in shining armor,
Will escort you into the arms of a carnival charmer.
Your Designer has dreamed much better for you,
Don't settle for a man who can't love you through and through.

MOM: THE SPIRITUAL MONITOR

Read: *RALIW* Chapter 10, pages 198-202 (Read
*Enhanced Heartbreak, Help to Emotionally Constrain a
Girl's Crushes,* and *Letter from Annie* sections.)

---

*H*elping to emotionally constrain our daughters
while they grow in patience is an emotional harness
that will protect them immeasurably throughout
high school and college and thereafter!

DAILY REFLECTION QUESTIONS

1. In what ways can you be a "spiritual monitor" for your daughter—specifically, in the area of dating and relationships? What does this look like and what does it protect your daughter from?

   - prayer + wisdom
   - don't be the cheer leader
   - speak out of godly wisdom

2. How can you as a mother and spiritual monitor help direct your daughter through "crushes" and the guys she "likes," preventing her from getting *carried away*?

encouraging her to wait in God's timing and for His will

3. What does the following statement mean to you? *"To raise a Lady in Waiting, one must be a Mother in Waiting."*

don't rush things even if they are dating a christian guy. don't make harmful jokes or comments about boy/girl friend relationship

DAILY PRAYER

Father, help me to be a Mother in Waiting. I know there is the tendency to speak certain ways about the boys (Daughter's Name) likes or has a crush on or is dating. Help me to choose my words wisely. I pray for increased discernment in this area.

Use me to be a spiritual monitor to my daughter without being pushy or coming off in the wrong way. Help her to know I sincerely care about her and want to see her make the absolute best decisions in her life. And God, continue to create a heart in (Daughter's Name) to pursue You in a deeper way. As You become her desire—more and more—I pray that patience becomes more and more natural for her.

In Jesus' Name, Amen.

PATIENCE PROTECTS

Read: *RALIW* Chapter 10, pages 202-206 (Read
Missed Out—While Waiting, Protected Not Rejected,
and *Impatient and Aggressive Girls* sections.)

---

*M*ay God allow you to clearly see that you
are a cheerleader for your daughter. One of
your common cheers needs to be, "Sweetie,
you are being protected, not rejected!"

DAILY REFLECTION QUESTIONS

1. What are the things that our daughters *miss out on* when they wait?
    How can you present these things to your daughter in a positive way,
    emphasizing the benefits of waiting?

    heart break, insecurities,
    sharing her heart with the wrong guy
    STD, pregnancy

2. How can you explain to your daughter that waiting *protects* and that
    lack of attention from boys (particularly the Bozos) is *not* rejection?

    It protects you from being hurt
    mentally, emotionally, physically, spiritually

3. What are some factors that drive girls toward being aggressive in their pursuit of relationships?

lusting with her eyes.
demanding spirits!
hunger in the heart for love
stir up sexual appitite
home without daddy.

DAILY PRAYER

Father, show (Daughter's Name) that waiting protects her and actually safeguards her for the one You have designed for her. Also, it saves her from the pain experienced by giving her heart away to the wrong guy.

Lord Jesus, I ask that You keep her heart safe. Also, help (Daughter's Name) to see why it is so important to protect that beautiful treasure and save it for the man who will also protect it.

In Jesus' Name, Amen.

SETTING BOUNDARIES IN ADVANCE

Read: *RALIW* Chapter 10, pages 206-209 (Read *Besides "Sixteen," What Other Dating Prep is Needed?*, *Who Owns Your Body?*, and *Vulnerable Situations Sexually* sections.)

---

*F*or any girl, young or not-so-young, the waiting period does not have to be wasted. The waiting for one's first date or one's first love is a time to evaluate your own personal strategy for moral purity.

DAILY REFLECTION QUESTIONS

1. How is the waiting period a time that does not have to be wasted for your daughter? What can she do during this time that will help prepare her for Boaz?

   Know who you are in Christ. develop moral character before you begin to date. establish limits ahead of time.

2. Why it is so important that your daughter establishes *clear boundaries* before she starts dating? How will this protect her for *when* she starts dating?

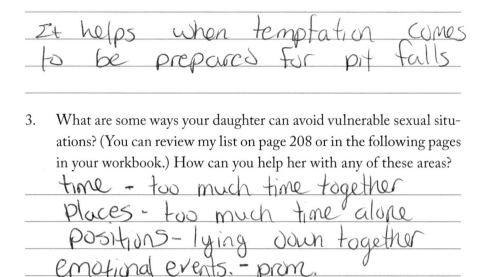

It helps when temptation comes to be prepared for pit falls

3. What are some ways your daughter can avoid vulnerable sexual situations? (You can review my list on page 208 or in the following pages in your workbook.) How can you help her with any of these areas?

time - too much time together
Places - too much time alone
positions - lying down together
emotional events. - prom.

DAILY PRAYER

Father, help me to be aware of what my daughter is doing, where she is going, and who she is with. I ask, Holy Spirit, that You give me wisdom and discernment. If anything she is doing or any person she is going to be with is not Your plan or purpose for her or might be destructive, I pray You would give me the wisdom and the ability to encourage her to not go. Also, train her ear to hear the Holy Spirit.

Help (Daughter's Name) establish solid boundaries now so that when she starts dating she knows where she stands. Give her grace to take a stand for purity that might be unpopular with her friends and that is definitely unpopular in this generation. May her pursuit not be popularity—may it be purity because of who she is in Christ.

In Jesus' Name, Amen.

JACKIE'S PRE-TEMPTATION PROGRAM

Prior to her first date, any young woman should know this list as well as she knows her home address. These points are like the markings on her moral compass. Before she goes out the door of your home with a young man, she should have these in her heart as pre-temptation preparation.

1.   How far would I go if Jesus were sitting next to me? (See Hebrews 4:13.)

2.   What would a person I respect think of me? (See 1 Timothy 4:12.)

3.   If we break up, can I look the other person in the eye? (See Acts 24:16.)

4.   Do I feel guilty? (See Psalms 38:4.)

5.   Does it turn me on sexually? (See First Peter 2:11.)

6.   Would I want my parents to see what I am doing? (See Colossians 3:20.)

7.   Would I want my future mate doing this right now? (See Hebrews 13:4.)

Day Five

WAITING FOR LOVE, REJECTING LUST

Read: *RALIW* Chapter 10, pages 209-212 (Read *Impatience: The Pen Writing Post-Dated Checks for Marital Unfaithfulness, Difference Between Lust and Love,* and *Patiently Waiting: How Will I Know It Is Him?* Sections.)

---

*T*he patience that you encourage in your girl's heart will allow her to wait for "true love." True love requires a maturity and commitment that impatience has no tolerance for.

DAILY REFLECTION QUESTIONS

1. How does remaining pure *before* marriage actually set the stage for a relationship that will not be compromised by adultery in the future?

_____

_____

_____

_____

2. What is your understanding of the differences between *lust* and *love*? How would you define each term? How does lust actually violate the definition of love that Paul provides in First Corinthians 13:4-5?

    _____

    _____

    _____

    _____

3. Surely, your daughter is asking the question: "How will I know it's him?" (referring to the appearance of her Boaz). What are some practical things you can share with her about *knowing* she has met the right guy?

    _____

    _____

    _____

    _____

DAILY PRAYER

Father, develop (Daughter's Name) into a Lady in Waiting who actually values that title. It is not a negative thing to her; instead, it is a badge of honor that she wears proudly. Continue to show her the value she possesses.

I know the day will come when (Daughter's Name) will meet Your best for her life. Help us to pray for him now so when the day comes, we are both ready. I pray You give her discernment to walk in Your perfect plan and that You give me grace to cheer her on.

In Jesus' Name, Amen.

TRUE LOVE LIST

Based on First Corinthians 13:4-8

- True love distinguishes between a person and a body.

- True love always generates respect.

- True love is self-giving.

- True love can thrive without physical expression.

- True love seeks to build relationship.

- True love embraces responsibility.

- True love can postpone gratification.

- True love is a commitment.

MOTHER/DAUGHTER SESSION

INSTRUCTIONS

You have both gone through Week 11 in the workbook (which covered Chapter 10 in the book). The focus of this week was patience. Here are some of the questions you can discuss during your mother-daughter session:

- Why has "wait" become such a bad word for so many young people?

- How does impatience actually set someone up to start *missionary dating*?

- What are the dangers of parents getting overly excited about the people their kids are dating? (This is why it is important to be a *Mother in Waiting*!)

- How can the *waiting process* actually protect someone from making bad decisions?

- What are some of the factors that cause women to be aggressive in pursuing guys?

- How does sticking to your convictions actually encourage you to be patient?

- In what ways can you avoid a vulnerable situation?

- How does pursuing purity *now* and waiting for God's best actually set someone up for a marriage that is not as likely to be compromised through adultery?

- What is your understanding of the difference between lust and love? What seems to be the more popular one in culture?

- What are some practical things you can do to help determine whether or not you have met the right guy?

This was your last mother/daughter session for this study. My prayer? That these dates continue long after you finish *Raising a Lady in Waiting*. I did not set this up merely to write a book. I told you, my vision is a movement. It's a lifestyle. It's a culture where mothers and daughters connect and benefit from each other.

I know age separates the two of you, but we need to push past that. Young people need the wisdom and experience from the older (I prefer the term *wiser*) generation, and we—yes, us wiser folks—need the vigor, passion, and energy of the young generation. When we link together, above all, in our family relationships, we literally set ourselves up to become world changers.

And thus, Week 11 concludes our time together.

On the heels of the last question, let me clarify—the "right guy" is *one* guy. Boaz is a husband, not a boyfriend or crush. Mom, be aware of this! Even after going through this book, your daughter might come home and be absolutely convinced she found Mr. Right. She may think he compliments all of the ideal guy traits on her list. Listen, there may be guys who are right guys, but not *her* right guy. Make sense? This is why it is so important not to jump the gun too soon. (Like writing her first name next to his last name *in seventh grade!*)

I encourage you—without sounding like I'm begging—to encourage your daughter to enjoy this season of her life. I live and breathe to see women actually make the most of the beautiful life God has given them. This is why I'm so "in your face" and honest about what I think about the topics we covered in our time together (I'm sure it didn't take long to figure that out). I want your daughter to take this time and enjoy it for what it is—a season in her life that she will never get back, but has the potential to shape the course of her future in the most wonderful ways imaginable!

Thanks a bunch for taking this journey with me.

And don't forget—you are your daughter's number one cheerleader and coach! Her friends aren't. The media can't be. School won't do it sufficiently. Church can't do it completely. It's *you!* I started with that reminder and I must end with it. This study was all about reminding her that you are *for* her. That is what I pray was communicated to her as you went through this study together. Even if she was reluctant or thought it would be lame or whatever. Mom, you are sowing seeds into her life that are going to produce a major harvest. Even if she did not seem receptive, I encourage you, trust the seed sown. God will water and cultivate it. He will do the work that you cannot.

Your job? Simply continue to be *for* your daughter. That is what all of these principles are purposed to do—arm you with the information to help lead her in the right direction.

Again, do what you can do. Refuse to compromise. Encourage her convictions. Say "no." Pray for her pursuit of Jesus. Be a listening ear. Model patience. All of that good stuff. But when it comes down to it, entrust her future to Jesus. He is so faithful, and I promise He loves your daughter more than you could even imagine. He is ever trustworthy and truly the greatest example she could set her eyes on! When your young lady in waiting and her King are tight, everything else will come into its place.

Running alongside you,

Jackie Kendall

Notes